W9-ABK-858

Twayne's English Authors Series

EDITOR OF THIS VOLUME

Sylvia E. Bowman

Indiana University

Henry Green

TEAS 235

Henry Green

HENRY GREEN

By KEITH C. ODOM

Texas Christian University

TWAYNE PUBLISHERS

A DIVISION OF G. K. HALL & CO., BOSTON

Copyright © 1978 by G. K. Hall & Co.
All Rights Reserved
First Printing

Library of Congress Cataloging in Publication Data

Odom, Keith.
  Henry Green.

(Twayne's English authors series; TEAS 235)
  Bibliography: pp. 148-51
  Includes index.
  1. Green, Henry, 1905-   —Criticism and interpretation.
I. Green, Henry, 1905-
PR6013.R416Z78   823'.9'12   77-18068
ISBN 0-8057-6706-1

For
Dennis and Clayton

Contents

About the Author

Keith C. Odom is Associate Professor of English and Director of the Honors Program at Texas Christian University. Since 1961 Dr. Odom has taught courses at Texas Christian University in the British novel, Russian and Scandinavian novels, the English Romantic period, and bibliography and methods of literary research. He is the author of articles and reviews published in *Descant, The CEA Critic, Studies in the Novel,* and other periodicals.

Dr. Odom graduated from East Central State College in 1952, then received his Masters degree in English from Oklahoma State University and his doctorate from the University of Wisconsin. He taught in the senior high school at Big Spring, Texas, and at Oklahoma State University, and the University of Wisconsin.

After discovering the novels of Henry Green in a graduate-school course, Dr. Odom continued his interest through further research and in his own graduate seminars. From Henry Green he was led into studies in symbolism and in other modern novelists. At the same time, he has continued his dissertation research interest in the Brontës and Romanticism.

Preface

On July 5, 1976, the weather in London was definitely not typical. In the depths of drought and heatwave, Mrs. Henry Yorke opened her door and welcomed my family and me to the home of Henry Green (Henry Vincent Yorke). The first-floor drawing room displayed the portrait, now well known to Green scholars, of Mr. Green in his red shirt and green jacket; and behind the drawing room was the small study with its large bookcase. Tacked onto the rear of the townhouse was a smaller television room, canted off at an angle, where Green spent much time in his last years watching sports events on television and frequently, because of his increasing deafness, turning the sound up so loud that the family closed the door for quiet. Our visit was an exciting but altogether pleasant occasion, in spite of the heat, for we sat and talked about the writings of Henry Green with his wife.

In somewhat the manner of Green's own oblique approach to situations, I begin by recalling the last important episode in my collection of material on Green in London in July 1976, just as Green decided that his (unwritten) story of World War II should begin in Cork in 1938 and that *Loving*, set at the height of that war, would take place in a fairy-tale castle in neutral Ireland. Green's unique vision of the world, which continues to interest readers of his novels, makes possible this critical-analytical study; for, though Green's last novel was published in 1952, subsequent book-length studies and critical articles affirm continued interest in his works, which are mostly still in print.

To survey all of the critical writing about Green's work is beyond the scope of this book, but a too-brief introduction that focused on one theme or one technique would not do justice to Green's canon. Because his works are too rich and versatile to be represented by one element only, I have developed a chronological survey of the books and most short works; and I emphasize Green's portrayal of the important periods of his life—youth, labor problems and depression, prewar fears, wartime, postwar austerity, and concerns for the future—and his major continuing themes—man's isolation, his quest for love as a solution to isolation, and the dissolution of society which Green saw and predicted throughout his lifetime from childhood in *Pack My Bag* to old age in *Concluding*. His ever-changing poetic prose style, which also remained uniquely his own, is discussed from a time of youthful lushness to the spare period of late middle age. The latter period ended in an attempt at the all-dialogue novel which climaxed his theoretical evolution but which provided him with not too much but too little opportunity to use his singular richness of descriptive imagery and his symbolic implication until he appeared to run out of things to say and interesting ways to say them almost simultaneously. Thus, if the reader wants a complete study in depth, this study is not the place to find it; but, if he seeks a detailed introduction to Green's major themes, techniques, characterizations, and styles and a more thorough than usual investigation of the pattern and consistency of his use of symbolism, linked with his realistic capture of the rhythms and words of everyday British speech, then this book, I sincerely hope, is the one he is seeking.

A note of caution is appropriate: if Green seems too oblique or impressionistic or if words naming symbolic objects occur in unrelated contexts or if characters are described as doing something or not doing something, don't hasten to decide that Green could not have meant what he said but instead must have intended something else entirely. We must beware. The words are there, and Green was the master of his words; and this supposed purveyor of insinuations and glancing reflections meant just what he said. Raunce and Edith in *Loving* did live happily ever after, and Charley in *Back* did commit himself to Nancy before he had forgotten his dead mistress, Rose. As Green told David Lambourne in an interview published in *Shenandoah* (Summer 1975), he wanted to remind his readers in every novel that, after his story ended, the characters arose the next day and life went on as before.

Visiting Henry Green's home was the culmination of an interest that began in the late 1950s, and I wish to thank his wife for her hospitality and enlightening conversation on that hot, dry July afternoon. Thanks must go also to Mr. John Lehmann, who discussed Green's work and Green the man with me several years before my London visit. My colleague Dr. Jim Corder, and my wife, Glenna, read my manuscript and made invaluable suggestions and criticisms. Mrs. Phyllis Drake and Mrs. Ruth Van Tine typed the book in various stages with patience, perseverance, and accuracy. I owe a debt of gratitude to all of them, and I acknowledge a wider debt to my graduate students who, through the years, found Green stimulating and in turn stimulated me. I can no more thank them all by name here, however, than I can the numerous others who helped, from librarians and colleagues at Texas Christian University to the used-book dealers who, unsolicited, loaned and even gave me several scarce Green items.

Texas Christian University   KEITH C. ODOM

Acknowledgments

I wish to thank the Viking Press and The Hogarth Press for permission to quote from books by Henry Green: *Living, Party Going, Pack My Bag,* and *Concluding*;

Henry Green for permission to quote from *Blindness*;

The Paris Review and Terry Southern for permission to quote from his interview of Henry Green; and

Descant and Texas Christian University for permission to incorporate into this book portions of my article "Symbolism and Diversion: Birds in the Novels of Henry Green."

Chronology

CHAPTER 1

The Two Worlds of Henry Green

H ENRY Green, a product of the English moneyed class before
World War I, does not deal with only his level of society, as he
shows in his first two novels, *Blindness* (1926) and *Living* (1929). Each
of these works portrays different social strata, the upper middle class
and the laboring class respectively; but *Living* also touches upon the
upper class—the world which Evelyn Waugh satirizes in *Vile Bodies*
(1930). Green demonstrates closer acquaintance with the gay young
moneyed set in his third novel, *Party Going* (1939), a work that
contains not only comic but also satiric aspects.

From *Pack My Bag* (1940) to *Doting* (1952), Green expands his
view of society even further. Without asserting a purely sociological
interpretation of his novels, I consider Green impressive because he
wrote authoritatively about several levels of British life. Affording
this broader view of the classes was the novelist Henry Green who
was also the industrialist Henry Vincent Yorke. Mr. Yorke and Mr.
Green were the same man, not just in terms of a *nom de plume*, but in
many other ways which become increasingly evident upon closer
examination. For instance, the observations and the experiences of
the industrialist provided indispensable material for the novelist.
Thus, even though biographical interpretation is not always the
firmest or the only basis for literary analysis, a certain amount is
necessary in this study of Mr. Green (Yorke), if not to emphasize
paradoxes then at least to clarify sources.

For most of every day, Henry Yorke was, for many years, an official
of H. Pontifex and Sons, "the family business, a medium-sized
engineering works in the Midlands, with its own iron and brass
foundries and machine shops."[1] After leaving Oxford at twenty-two,
he began work in one of the shops and eventually became the
company's managing director. The fact that he came from a moneyed
family and always lived in financial security, however, bears on his
attitudes toward novelistic art. He did not need to be concerned

about the commercial success of a novel; writing was not his principal occupation.

Henry Green felt free to experiment as he pleased and to follow whatever novelistic technique appeared most advisable. But though this freedom was partially a result of his business connections, which he felt, by the way, were necessary to the survival of the modern artist, Green kept his life as a writer separated as much as possible from his life as a businessman. The novelist in him formed the habit of writing about a thousand words a day at work during his lunch hour and at home after dinner.[2]

Green jealously preserved his private life apart from his literary life, but he appeared in literary circles; and he did so more frequently in the 1950s than before. His friends included such writers as Evelyn Waugh, Christopher Isherwood, W. H. Auden, John Lehmann, and V. S. Pritchett. Without wanting to, as he stated repeatedly, Green inevitably linked both sides of his life and became an unusual modern artist, one who was engaged in commerce with the business world but one who still created the private world, the imaginative life, necessary to the novelist. He did not consider his writing to be unusual, but natural. "I write books," he comments in *Pack My Bag*, "but I am not proud of this any more than anyone is of their nails growing . . . (238)."

I   *Green and the Critics*

Critics differ in their interpretations of Green's artistic aims and attitudes as being, for instance, objective or cold; indeed, both Philip Toynbee and Martin Greenberg have called him a "cold fish." Edward Stokes states that "from the beginning [Green] has aimed at (and now insists on) a strict objectivity and self-suppression."[3] The basis of this statement is partly Green's own comment that "the writer . . . has no business with the story he is writing. . . ."[4] In any case, Anthony Quinton is "inclined to doubt that the human condition in general is of much interest or even meaningful to Henry Green."[5] Philip Toynbee sees "no compassion in Green's vision." "Perhaps," Toynbee adds, "it is by this fact that his achievement can be both understood and 'placed.' It is both his strength and his limitation."[6]

Other critics, however, think that Green does not lack compassion. V. S. Pritchett believes that at least *Back, Loving*, and *Party Going* have compassion and sensibility, but he thinks that these qualities "are cut down in *Nothing* and *Doting*."[7] According to James Hilton, "*Concluding* is a novel of imagination and compassion."[8] Green kept out of his novels, however, by viewing the action as from the ceiling, as Philip Toynbee would have it, or as being present "only in solution, and not by proxy."[9]

None of the varying interpretations necessarily constitutes bad criticism or indicates that Green wrote badly. Most critics are favorable in their estimates of Green as a novelist. Also, while purporting to analyze the novels themselves and asserting that Green is not "in" his novels, most critics cannot keep away from the subject of Henry Green. A basic focus of his works is involved here, one that the critics ignore by insistence upon his complete absence from the novels. Dealing with a problem related to objectivity, Edward Stokes speaks for many critics when he says that none of Green's works "is autobiographical in substance: even in *Living* and *Caught* no character is a *persona* or mask for Green himself." Nevertheless, Green is "inevitably present in his work" as is every novelist, at least in "the qualities that make up his special vision."[10] Green's novels are clearly his, though they often differ in subject matter.

II   *Green the Chronicler*

The assertion that Green stays out of his novels is not unanimous.[11] Many critics have not forgotten the autobiographical work, *Pack My Bag,* which Green wrote at the beginning of World War II. What Green created in that case was only an explicit exercise of what he did before and after: he wrote out of his own experiences. While Green wrote no explicit autobiography containing himself as a character except *Pack My Bag,* he developed a running autobiography of sorts throughout his novels and faithfully recorded his own times in them. He reveals an important focus of his vision in response to Terry Southern's question whether two of his "novels, *Blindness* and *Pack My Bag* are . . 'autobiographical.' " He answers, "Yes, those two are mostly autobiographical. But where they are about myself, they are not necessarily accurate as a portrait; they aren't photographs. After all, no one knows what he is like, he just tries to give some sort of picture of his time."[12] More broadly, however, he provides this picture in all of his novels.

Consonant with this personal, if not purely autobiographical, orientation, Green discovers his themes and theses in the problems of man that are basically universal but are particularly related to the problems encountered during Green's own life. Modern man, perhaps more than ever before, finds himself alone in the world; and his very nature makes him dissatisfied with this condition. He must seek relationships, often without knowing or feeling that others are also interested in such relationships. Edward Stokes states that "it would not be a gross oversimplification to say that the basic theme of Green's work is that of love versus loneliness." Earlier, however, Stokes prepared for this statement with his remark that "in all his books, while preserving verisimilitude of surface, Green connects his contemporary characters and situations with universal and timeless emotions, and with man's perennial predicaments and perplexities, the most important of which, for Green, is the problem of human happiness and how it is to be attained."[13] Primarily, man seeks happiness, not the kind ultimately satisfied by mere association or even by friendship but the kind completed by love.

Thus in Green's novels characters seek love or something akin to it, however wrong-headed or inept rather than fulfilling it may be. As a result Green, like others before him, must stipulate that his characters gain some understanding of themselves as a necessary aid to achieving love. Green provides enough evidence of this stipulation in his novels to support the hypothesis that "in each of the novels of Henry Green one or more characters adopt, relinquish, or neglect an available program of action and suffering which leads to self-creation." The hypothesis "links precepts and discovers structure (or perhaps a reason for the impairment of structure) in each novel and consonance in the novels as a whole."[14] Augmenting the difficulty of this self-learning process is growth and the necessity for new knowledge at each stage in a person's life. Most of Green's characters, ironically, are like people in general; they are not particularly introspective, not always very sensitive, not even very intelligent. Nonetheless, they solve their problems as best they can.

Further complicating man's quest for happiness and especially interesting to Green throughout his career are the difficulties involving man in the mass, the social structures within or outside which all men must live. Since World War I, society has changed, sometimes slowly and sometimes almost too swiftly for man to assimilate. Green illustrates these rapid developments by the labor-management problems in different ways in *Living, Loving,* and *Concluding;* the chaos and change of war in *Caught* and *Back;* and the dissolving underpinnings of high society in *Party Going, Nothing,* and *Doting.*

Green, throughout his writing career, deals with the theme of dissolution in terms of people rather than in those of strict philosophical, psychological, sociological, or religious theories. Religion, in particular, never figures in his novels. He does not allow himself such a committed viewpoint, for he accepts the existing world and makes his characters function in it. Green is socially aware, even in the critical sense; but, when he was asked whether social awareness is a responsibility of the writer, he answered, "The writer must be disengaged or else he is writing politics."[15] Green is a literary artist, not a sociopolitical writer. Any commentary Green makes comes, for the most part, obliquely through suggestion, metaphor, symbolism, and allusion. Even the two novels with strong proletarian themes, *Living* and *Party Going*, achieve their effects through such poetic rather than through explicit and prosaic means.

Green's personal independence and individual artistic vision contribute to his originality as a novelist. Reading his novels is an experience in discovering new territory, for few of his passages bring to mind another novelist. Subsequent readings must be handled carefully, however; for Green may evoke with fleeting glimpses or with oblique hints too many other writers like C. M. Doughty, Virginia Woolf, and Ivy Compton-Burnett. Certainly, a few writers influenced Green; but he was neither the follower nor the leader of a literary school.

CHAPTER 2

The Novel Theorist

ALTHOUGH Green revealed his conscious interest in the art of the novel by commenting that all of his novels form "an advanced attempt to break up the old-fashioned type of novel,"[1] his success in this attempt is debatable. His comment is not an espousal of literary nihilism but an assertion that his practice is backed by theory. He has stated some of his theory formally; some of it critics have deduced; and the critics' attempts to interpret his theoretical pronouncements are interesting and helpful but often complex. In an introductory study of Green, a preferable approach is to consider the writings in which he first broaches his critical opinions and to attempt a synthesis. His statements are clearer when placed both in context and in synthesized interrelationship with each other. This literal approach gains a more exact appraisal of what Green himself says and allows fuller illustration, in later chapters, of what he does.

I The Oblique Approach

Green did not publish most of his critical pronouncements until 1950 and 1951. He must have had his ideas long before; but, since *Nothing* and *Doting* were published at about the same time, the first reaction was to apply Green's theories only to them. Relevance to Green's entire canon, however, becomes more obvious as we read his articles on novel theory and then add such hints as Green provides elsewhere in his work or in interviews.

Green's novelistic theories are not unusual except for his emphasis on dialogue. He develops his nonrepresentational theory, one transferred from visual art to the novel,[2] by involving what he calls an oblique approach to his scenes that is effected through limited descriptive language and, especially, through dialogue. Green cites two advantages to be gained in communication of author to reader by using dialogue for narrative purposes: "that we do not have time to define what we mean in conversation and . . . we thereby arrive easier at a general conventional understanding of what is being said," and that we understand dialogue more readily because present-day communications are more often oral than written.[3] His prediction that for a time at least the future of narrative lay in dialogue elicited rejection by C. P. Snow, who said flatly that Green was "hopelessly confused." Commenting in particular on Green's essay "The English Novel of the Future," Snow wrote that, though Green says "some true and penetrating things. . . . they do not all add up; in the end one is left thinking that the novel Mr. Green predicts certainly will not happen, and that it would be a minor horror if it did."[4] Subsequent novelists have not borne out Green's predictions about the dialogue novel fully; but, while his *Nothing* and *Doting* are not major novels, they are written as closely as possible to follow his credo; and they are not minor horrors, either.

Green, like most novelists, desires to communicate with the reader. His major preoccupation clearly is with the success and failure of communication. Instead of facilitating an ideal situation for communication, however, he emphasizes not only man's individuality but also his solitariness. That Green deliberately prevents his characters from communicating is to an extent a result of his own deafness and of what he had learned from it, both as a help and a hindrance. As he told Alan Ross, "I have as I think short-circuited communication but because I'm so deaf I don't know if I've done it well."[5]

Green carries his theories further, however, than the Chekhovian tendency of his characters to converse on different subjects and at cross-purposes. He stresses the ambiguity of art, stating that "a novel should be all things to all men, if only because the reaction of each individual reader varies in each case."[6] Thus he extends ambiguity to the communication between writer and reader because of the ambiguity of life itself and because of the belief that prose fiction in the future should not be clear but loaded with a poetic sort of implication which provides something for everyone.

Complex as this concept may appear, Green develops the idea still further, by stating that the "quality of every good book" is to challenge at once the attention, hold it, and draw everyone "into a communion of people, each, in his own way, equally interested in what would happen next."[7] Green is not trying to create stage drama or even real-life conversation; his interest is in "the unspoken communication between novelist and reader in narrative and not about that which may exist between a speaker and his audience, or even between husband and wife, in life." In this case, Green does not include reading aloud; to him, "reading is a kind of unspoken communion with print."[8] Thus he comes to believe more in the importance of written dialogue and less in the efficacy of description.

The novel is, therefore, a creation of something living between the writer and reader through dialogue. Presentation of a theme creates communication between writer and reader; dialogue in real life contains a large measure of humor; and humor, then, must be what draws writer and reader together.[9] Humor aids the writer in communicating with the reader, Green told Terry Southern, by relaxing the characters, by luring the reader further into the novel, and by effecting a communion of author and audience.[10] Characters must not interrupt their true-to-life dialogues to interpret to the reader what the writer means. Each writer must choose his own theme from within himself and not from any exterior source. But disaster or tragedy is no longer the writer's way to a communion with the reader; humor, the happy ending, the continuing life and characters after the novel has ended are today's methods.

Along with communion and communication, Green also believed in the provocativeness of what is left unsaid and in man's innate fascination with words. The child feels this fascination as he learns words which are progressively more difficult and which have an increasing number of meanings. Context, therefore, is important since words have so many meanings; and they must be communicative enough not to need explanatory intrusions by either the author or his characters. At the same time, the writer cannot allow his style to become static and to develop clichés from which he cannot escape.[11] The strength of his desire to communicate with his reader urged Green into a preoccupation with semantics.

The novelist paints with words. In nonrepresentational painting, the artist works with color, design, and arrangement; and they may lead to "a harmonious whole which may have little direct relation to nature."[12] For the novelist, words are colors and tones; and the placement of characters is the design and the composition that provide the context of the story. With the nonrepresentational theory, Green, admitting that a fictional character is "a life which isn't," attempts to "create life in the reader which cannot eat, drink or procreate, but which can die. . . ." Nonrepresentational techniques of character placement involving "the superimposing of one scene on another, or the telescoping of two scenes into one," must then be utilized to achieve "substance and depth."[13]

"The oblique approach" and "the crabwise approach" are terms closely related to the nonrepresentational concept: *oblique* applies more precisely to his juxtaposition or superimposition of scenes and to his use of indirection and misunderstanding in dialogue.[14] The scene in *Loving* in which Mrs. Tennant attempts to discuss the theft of her ring with Mrs. Welch, the cook, who babbles on about the drains, criminality among the servants, and her stolen waterglass is an example of both the nonrepresentational concept and the oblique approach.

II   *Narrative through Dialogue*

Green did not arrive at narrative through dialogue late in his career. In his first novel, *Blindness*, dialogue carries much of the narrative. The most concise statement of Green's theory in 1950 was, therefore, applicable to all of his fiction: "if you want to create life the only way not to set about it is by explanation. No, it is in the various ways the same thing can be put that lies the power and wonder of dialogue, the glory of the language."[15] Green expands his statement with inclusion of other more esthetic complexities. For instance, he still has reference to the silent communication of spoken conversation from writer to reader, not the simple reproduction of literal speech.

Green's considerable attention to English talk is evidenced not only by his sensitive estimate of James Sutherland's selections in *The Oxford Book of English Talk* but also by his own ideas. At one point in his review of the book, for example, Green declares that "written dialogue is not like the real thing, and can never be."[16] This statement, too, is related to his idea that dialogue in a novel is as different from real conversation as the communication between a writer and his reader is different from that between a speaker and his audience. Green defines talk as "an exchange between two or more people watching the expression on each other's faces, hearing the tone of voice. Perhaps there is . . . endless repetition. Certainly there are pauses, hesitations, and changes of direction which will never do in print."[17]

Again he is preoccupied with semantics: "that great source of our language as we know it, the spoken word, out of which, as the language changes from generation to generation the written word springs; new turns of phrase as they come up in speech, being the tools of the poet and the novelist."[18] Green, then, was not spinning ideas out of cobwebs in his head; he thought long and deeply about the English language. He was not only listening to multitudes speak but also discovering the patterns, rhythms, and meanings which actually bind one person to another in an understanding communion.

Giorgio Melchiori appraises Green's esthetic use of colloquial speech as an attempt "to strike a balance between the realistic rendering of common conversation and the underlying secret rhythmical pattern which gives at times poignancy and musical beauty to the speech of the uncultured."[19] That Green succeeds so well vindicates, to a degree, his dialogue theory in spite of C. P. Snow's skepticism and the lessened force of the two dialogue novels, *Nothing* and *Doting.*

Besides having an uncanny ear for real conversation, Green draws upon dramatic sources for his dialogue theory. Though he denies drama as an artistic medium in order to eliminate actors as interpretive middlemen, Green did write a play which was not produced. He writes scenes which in their unity of action and dependence on a dialogue show a knowledge of techniques from not only the stage but also the cinema. *Living* and *Loving,* particularly, contain cinematic close-ups and scene shifts which break his narratives into smaller units than earlier novelists employed.

Green does not contradict himself by involving his oblique approach with any type of drama. He describes the involvement when differentiating between novelistic art and journalistic craft. The journalist much be as direct as possible, whereas the novelist must achieve obliquity because "in life the intimations of reality are nearly always oblique." To Green one can learn more from a person's lie than from his truth, and when there are "no direct answers in dialogue," verisimilitude results.[20] The crabwise approach is needed because, as Green says, "people strike sparks off each other, that is what I try to note down. But mark well, they only do this when they are talking together."[21] Real people, then, are naturally oblique when they talk; and Green believes that the novelist must not only produce crabwise conversation to be realistic but also use this realistic method to communicate with his reader through his characters' conversations. An example, of which Green expressed pride, is a crucial conversation in *Back* between Charley Summers and his landlady when she must tell him three things important to him and to the story; but she does so by almost classic obliquity (32–34).

Admitting that an entire novel cannot be written exclusively in dialogue, Green had to make decisions about how much description and stage direction would be necessary and could be allowed; ideally, little of either. The solution to his problems Green found, again, in the reader, whose imagination he sought to rekindle in each new scene by providing just enough stage direction to designate the speaker and his essential action and by allowing anyone who could speak to do so while the reader provided the details. From his beginnings in *Blindness* with its lush Edwardian descriptions, Green worked gradually to reduce the amount of everything except dialogue. His tendency was toward alternate blocks of dialogue and description with occasional outbursts of dazzling color and imagery that reached a climax in *Loving*. *Nothing* and *Doting* virtually are all dialogue-plus-stage directions; but some vivid description occurs in scenes like the nightclub performances in *Doting*.

Green partially justifies using so much dialogue through his claims about point of view. He implies that the author's speaking to and about his characters from somewhere in one corner of the ceiling is an unrealistic technique. Instead, he expects the writer to "keep any direct statement from himself out of his narrative because anything of the kind has an inhibiting effect on the magic which has to be created between writer and reader."[22] Such an idea consists of more than Isherwood's "I am a camera" technique in *Goodbye to Berlin*.

By asserting that the novelist should stay outside, uninvolved, Green does not intend journalistic depersonalization. Since the novelist must "inspire a concious act of imagination in the reader," whereas the journalist's aim is different, the novelist must be "extremely personal in narrative." But, whenever a novelist begins narrating a story, he is trying to create interest in himself, not in the characters. Since "we learn almost everything in life from what is done after a great deal of talk," we learn most about the characters in a novel through dialogue. The crux of his idea is that people probably cannot know in real life "what other people are really like." Even more definitely, he says "We certainly do not know what other people are thinking and feeling. How then can the novelist be so sure?"[23] A traditional reply to Green's question is that the novelist can be sure of what his characters are thinking and feeling because he invented them and must know virtually all there is to know about them.

Nevertheless, Green, who employs third-person point of view almost exclusively, except in *Pack My Bag*, does not limit the narrative to only one character's thoughts; but neither is he the traditional omniscient author. The characters must reveal themselves to the reader through conversation, though even they do not always recognize such self-revelation. In *Back*, for instance, the landlady, Mrs. Frazier, reveals her selfishness when she denies having enough coal to heat Charley Summers's room (31—32). This attempt to have characters in a novel show themselves mostly by implication, with little or no authorial comment, may be confusing for a time but should eventually become significant to the reader; but Green's fulfillment of his objective may be as much a challenge for the reader as for the participants in the dialogue.

Although Green is admitting the basic realism of his characters, whom he knows from his own experience, he also knows that impressions of people can be misleading. In *Pack My Bag*, for instance, he marvels at "how wonderful they seem the first few times. . ., how well it all goes and then how dull it becomes and flat" (63–64). Green, however, is involved with his characters in an unusual sense. He takes a personal interest in what occurs from a point outside the story; he allows his characters to be themselves and to go their own way while showing that he understands, sympathetically, all dimensions of human nature. Mrs. Frazier pays no penalty for her selfishness and duplicity.

III   *A Doughty Stylist*

Philip Toynbee, calling Green a "terrorist of language," declares that he is a self-conscious, mannered, and, at the same time, most natural writer.[24] Green, however, is not self-conscious but conscious; and his writing is not mannered in the strict sense of the word. True, Green utilizes elements of style that recur, such as his redundant use of coordinate conjunctions, his tendency to use short sentences, or his even more noticeable metaphorical uses of birds and flowers. But he also varies his style to fit the circumstances in a particular novel, and his style has undergone development from *Blindness* to *Doting*. When Alan Ross once asked him whether he achieved his style with an "ideal reader in mind," he replied, "I write for about six people (including myself) whom I respect and for no one else."[25]

No matter what is said about Green's syntax or sentence structure, his style should not be considered undignified. A possible influence upon his stylistic dignity is *Travels in Arabia Deserta* (1888), by Charles M. Doughty, the subject of Green's extremely favorable critical article. Among Green's comments about Doughty as a writer is the significant statement that "it is not hard to break through Doughty's convention to the character of the man beneath, indeed his style is so perfectly the expression of his personality that he stands out as though in the harsh sunlight he describes."[26] A decade later, when rejecting dialect in the future novel, Green makes an exception for "dialect [that] is consciously used poetically, as in the inventive and entirely successful Arabian English of Doughty."[27] Green's dialogue, of course, is everyday English speech, not Arabian English; but the dialogue of both writers betrays their keen ears for the everyday conversation of their characters.

Other possible influences on Green's style, which he does not mention but which are evident enough, are the King James Bible and Anglo-Saxon.[28] In *Living*, the King James Bible resounds in a sentence like "Women gave them to eat" (108); and, in *Nothing*, the Anglo-Saxon influence shows in sentences which are compressed and emphatic with repetition maintained by alliteration and assonance; for example, "Gold scrolls over white soup plates sparkled clean in the park's sun without" (13). Green shows from his comments about style that he wants to be taken seriously and that he reserves to himself the decision about appropriate style in any given novel. Possible influence by or affinity with other writers such as George Moore, who repeatedly revised and polished the prose in his novels, must not obscure Green's supreme originality.

IV *Those Mysterious Symbols*

Critics have been confused and sometimes downright contradictory about whether Green's complex uses of objects are solidly symbolic or simply and tantalizingly suggestive. Though William York Tindall lists Henry Green among the writers of symbolist novels in his *Forces in Modern British Literature*, he admits elsewhere his inability to tie Green's symbolic objects to any exact meaning. About *Loving* he writes, "unexhausted, the 'great consult' of glancing images and rhythms continues to issue rays, perceptible to others perhaps or to me at another time."[29] In an essay published earlier than Tindall's comments, Walter Allen stated in one sentence that Green's use of pigeons in *Living* is symbolic and in the next that this use is "something approaching symbolism."[30] Though the difficulties of interpreting Green's novels continue, agreement that the writing is symbolic has increased. Looking at this problem with Green's few statements about it in mind should clarify matters somewhat.

Besides the mystery and implication common in Green's novels, probably the greatest single influence in interpreting and resolving Green's use of symbolism is his statement in *Pack My Bag*. "Prose," he wrote, "is not to be read aloud but to oneself alone at night, and it is not quick as poetry but rather a gathering web of insinuations which go further than names however shared can ever go" (88). Naturally critics seized upon that fascinating phrase "a gathering web of insinuations" as the explanation for Green's abstruseness. The reader is not to understand Green; instead, he should admire all that "cross-flickering," all those "random beauties" or all these "glancing reflections."

Two elements of the quotation should be emphasized, however. First, Green is explaining the nature of prose in his own inimitable manner; and his statement can apply as much to the prose of others as to his own. Second, the sentence is part of a statement that relates why Green would not use actual names in the autobiographical work he was writing. "Prose," Green continues in *Pack My Bag*, "should be a long intimacy between strangers with no direct appeal to what both may have known. It should slowly appeal to feelings unexpressed, it should in the end draw tears out of the stone, and feelings are not bounded by the associations common to place names or to persons with whom the reader is unexpectedly familiar" (88). The idea expressed is itself quite interesting, but it is not about symbolism but about the use of names in prose.

When Terry Southern finally did ask Green, "What do you say about the use of symbolism?" Green's answer was in effect an admission that he used it; but what he said followed two fiction theories that he had already elucidated in his own literary articles. First, he employed the crabwise approach by answering Southern by asking more questions: "You can't escape it can you? What after all is one to do with oneself in print?" Second, he repeated the idea that a novelist should be all things to all readers, or to as many as possible: "Surely the only way to cover all these readers is to use what is called symbolism."[31] Green leaves his readers to decide not whether he uses symbolism but how he does it and what it means.

In general, Green employs two classes of objects most frequently as symbols: birds and flowers. "Birds evidently represent flight, the urge towards independence, the individual as opposed to the social impulses. Flowers mean the opposite: return, and some sense of identification with society."[32] Other interpretations are possible upon close examination of, for example, the dead pigeon which predicts the demise of the frivolous upper class in *Party Going*. Even if Giorgio Melchiori requires a symbol to possess "precision of reference and consistency,"[33] Green provides some mystery when he both utilizes symbols consistently and creates diversions by using the same words (birds, flowers, and the like) in everyday dialogue and description from which the reader must sort his symbolic uses. These diversions can be considered facets of both Green's artistic independence and his humor.

These theories of the novel indicate that Green has been very much the conscious artist. Certainly his writing is individual, resembling no other novelist completely, though it is not utterly unique. His theories are not completely new for many modern novelists use nonrepresentational techniques. Even his extreme use of dialogue finds resemblances in Anthony Powell's *Afternoon Men,* George V. Higgins's *The Friends of Eddie Coyle,* and all of Ivy Compton-Burnett's novels. Uniqueness, however, is not so important as achievement. Green's considerable success can be shown by thorough examinations of his works in the following chapters.

CHAPTER 3

Beginning

A S a first novel, *Blindness* (1926) is impressive; as a novel by a schoolboy, it is astonishing. Just into his twenties, Green moved ahead of other members of his generation who would become famous. Evelyn Waugh, for instance, did not publish *Decline and Fall* until 1928, the same year as Christopher Isherwood's *All the Conspirators*. The next year Graham Greene published *The Man Within*; and Henry Green's schoolfellow, George Orwell, did not publish *Down and Out in Paris and London* until 1933, or *Burmese Days* until 1934. *Blindness*, however, was not merely a first for a new generation; it pointed to some of the future concerns of the adult world with which the later novels would deal. Also, Green was indicating in this first novel the beginning of several of the thematic and artistic routes he was to follow during the next twenty-six years.

The sureness of Green's independence and his sense of artistry contributed to his choosing a subject both difficult to develop and painful to read. The accidental blinding of a talented schoolboy who is drawn to the visual arts and who has plans for a literary career and then must adjust himself to permanent darkness—such a subject was not the most hopeful for pleasing the mass reading public in 1926. As Green notes in *Pack My Bag*, he began to write his first novel at Eton, where he had the added encouragement of his school society of arts; continued it in France; and finished it at Oxford. John Buchan, author and family friend, read the manuscript and told Green that he would "never make an author."[1] Some weeks later, however, Green received a letter from Buchan suggesting that he call on Edward Garnett, the publisher's reader who handled Buchan's work. Garnett took Green in hand and, using his technique of flattery and then advice, showed the young novelist how to write dialogue and narrative. Such enviable assistance helps to explain the early appearance of *Blindness*.

Publication did not exactly launch Green as a new literary star; for though there was some critical fanfare, it was muted. Still, the later custom of saying that reviewers lightly dismissed the book is too extreme. A contemporary reviewer wrote that "one is troubled by the imaginative power of this tragic tale . . . ." To another critic, the "young Englishman has produced an unusual and compelling book" and it is "thoroughly worth noticing."[2] Both reviews (admittedly there seems not to have been a great many more) used words like "subtle", "penetrating", and "admirable"—not terms of light dismissal. In spite of Green's restraint, polish, and objectivity—rare enough in a first and early novel—critics have paid less attention to *Blindness* than it merits.

From this beginning novel, Green shows the personal orientation from which he writes about problems and situations in important periods of his life. When the novel was first published, D. W. Brogan expressed suspicion that the young man responsible may have been both subject and author. Green later acknowledged that both *Blindness* and *Pack My Bag* are autobiographical. His application of the term "autobiographical" is useful for what it reveals about the main character, John Haye, and for what Green was able to see in him. Green was not interested in fictionalized autobiography; the artist in him was already making judgments about literary propriety—and synthesis.

In a qualified sense Green was writing a *Bildungsroman*, portraying the growth of an adolescent into maturity. The hint of autobiography, about as overt as Green ever gets, occurs in a first section exclusively comprising selections from John Haye's diary. What Green says about his own school days in *Pack My Bag*—the society of arts, preparations for a literary career, personal experiences, and intellectual ideas—indicates a close similarity to the schoolboy in *Blindness*. His own experience is only a source of the young author's insight into the character; for Green goes beyond, into realms where he must be creative.

Beginning with a boy he knows, Green uses sympathetic restraint to deal with John Haye's maturation. He is not satisfied with the usual middle-class problems, however, such as the first blooming and fading of adolescent love, though John finds Joan Entwhistle and develops an independent relationship with her. Instead, Green constructs a more complex situation, physically and emotionally, of the sensitive and artistic youth who must accept permanent blindness and then begin his life anew. He persuades his stepmother to move them to London for his new life, and he leaves an insensitive Joan to

care for her degenerate father. Green's choice of blindness for plot
complication allowed him an early excuse to employ his own recep-
tiveness to sounds, his "celebrated ear," and his own "celebrated
deafness." With sure comprehension Green portrays, therefore, the
problems of the handicapped person, both his pain and subsequent
accommodation and the pain which his handicap inflicts upon others.

I *Themes*

The immediately obvious theme of *Blindness* involves this handicap and the victim's fight to overcome it at the same time that he
might achieve maturity. The accidental blinding of John Haye contains an element of poetic justice; for, as we learn from his diary, he is
something of a bully and even more of a snob, but not more of one
than many boys of his age and with his artistic interests. The
important aspect of his situation is his readjustment and reconcilia-
tion that finally ends in a flash of sublimation amounting to victory.
After being deprived of sight, he progresses to an appreciation of the
sounds of voices, birdsongs, and finally bells which he learns to utilize
in a fulfilling manner. He also learns more about himself; he progresses from figurative darkness of immaturity to literal darkness and
from that to the figurative light of self-knowledge, which he finds
more important that the literal light of sight.

This notion of human growth or "self-creation," which A. Kingsley
Weatherhead has examined in detail, is a continuing theme throughout Green's works. But, beyond the immediate theme lie at least
three other important themes. The most obvious theme is loneliness,
because it involved not only the isolation of a blinded boy but also that
of the alcoholic, unfrocked minister, Mr. Entwhistle, who has so
withdrawn from the pains and the frustrations of life that he has no
hope of ever returning to close intercourse with humanity or God. A
second and related theme is man's search for love and happiness.
Again John's problems are obvious, and his first attempt at solution,
the foredoomed involvement with Joan, forms the middle section of
the novel. Joan herself daydreams of the young farmer who would
satisfy her need for physical love; but she, like Mrs. Haye, has at least
some happiness in her life which satisfies her no matter how disagree-
able the reader may find it. Herein lies some of the strength of the two
women in the novel. Mr. Entwhistle's troubles were caused by his
frustrated quest for love and happiness: his wife withheld love; and
his extravagance lost him the happiness from his roses.

A third theme, the one which indicates the broad social significance of Green's novels, is social dissolution; but this concern is less obvious in *Blindness* than in later novels. There is a sense of social dissolution in the moral decay and ostracism of Mr. Entwhistle, but this traditional situation Green could discover in both Victorian and Georgian fiction. The significant change comes in the action of John Haye when he breaks tradition by selling the family estate instead of retreating to it as a blind gentleman farmer. He and his stepmother move to the city, leaving, Mrs. Haye fears, the dependent village of Barwood without proper guidance and control. Thematically, then, Green's first novel contains many of the most important elements of his mature novels.

II *Early Style*

The greatest difference between *Blindness* and Green's later novels is in style, but we do discover some hints of the prose stylist to follow. In *Blindness*, Green employed poetic prose which he was later to use more sparingly, as he did in *Loving*. In *Pack My Bag*, he admits amusement about his more elaborate and conventional passages; but he is also proud of the improvement between his earlier diary entries and his passages in *Blindness*, for example: "He was alone for the moment. Nan had left him to take a cup of tea. The nurse was taking the daily walk that was necessary to her trade union health, and Mrs. Haye had gone up to the village to console Mrs. Trench, whose week-old baby was dying" (80). As an early reviewer commented, *Blindness* is "expressed in a clear and flexible prose."[3] Green already wrote the prose style which he would adapt and control throughout his novels, for he adjusted the simplicity or the complexity to fit the occasion.

In *Blindness*, as Walter Allen states, "the writing, the descriptions of nature in which the book abounds, are Georgian: Rupert Brooke is just around the corner and John Drinkwater may drop in at any moment."[4] Allen probably alluded to the frequency with which the English countryside appeared in Georgian poetry and to the milder irony of writing before the middle of World War I when disillusionment set in. An interesting similarity appears between the following passage from *Blindness* and descriptions of natural things in, for instance, Rupert Brooke's poem "Heaven" (1913):

> The day would draw away as if sucked down in the
> east, where a little rose made as if to play with

> pearl and grey and blue. There were chub he had
> missed, four or five he would have caught, and more
> further on. A kingfisher might shoot out to dart
> down the river, a guilty thing in colours. . . .
> He would go on, casting his fly. . . . (83–84)

Brooke's poem tells of "Fish (fly-replete, in depth of June, / Dawdling away their wat'ry noon)" and of their gently satiric hope for a world in which there "Is wetter water, slimier slime!"[5]

However, Green's descriptions and the literary allusions in *Blindness* are more extensive and lush than in his other novels. The literary allusions seem to contribute to the characterization of John Haye; for he, like Green, is a voracious reader. A brief survey shows the following authors mentioned in John's diary in order of appearance: Thomas Carlyle (three times), Charlotte Brontë, Nikolai Gogol, Winston Churchill (his biography), Robert Browning (and the artist Vincent Van Gogh, on the same page), George Moore, Fyodor Dostoevsky, and Ivan Turgenev. Adding a note of youthful insouciance to John's personality is an enthusiastic entry about *Potash and Perlmutter* by Montague Glass, the humorist. Other choices which are serious, romantic, poetic, or psychological indicate the breadth of John's reading.

Later novels are far less allusive; most of Green's characters, except for John Haye, are unintellectual. Another reason for Green's eliminating literary allusion involves serious artistic decisions. John Russell reports that in 1926 Green was already concerned about getting "too bound up in artifacts," that is, other authors' works. In some notes on remembering, he mentioned the goal of "*general* recollection"; and he disparaged "remembering by quotation" and approved "remembering by the significant irrelevance."[6] This goal is characteristic of Green's independent artistic temperament and is also prophetic of his later emphasis on the oblique or crabwise approach.

Description in *Blindness* is elaborated by images which, as we have noted, Green finds irresistible—flowers and birds. Flowers, especially roses, relate in the novel directly to most of the characters and aid in their character development (or deterioration in the case of Mr. Entwhistle). Birds, however, are the most abundant manifestations of nature in this novel, as in several others. In *Blindness*, there are almost as many birds as in *Loving* or *Concluding;* for at least fifty-six pages of the two hundred fifty-four in *Blindness* mention birds: rooks, chickens, pigeons, partridges, sparrows, and starlings. They create atmosphere, as when "a blackbird warned as he fled down wind" (151). They aid in the description of setting, as do the chickens around the Entwhistle house; but most importantly, they tend to follow John Haye's development from adolescent callowness through blindness to adjustment. The particular kind of bird does not matter so much as how it changes John's attitude toward nature, which he now must hear rather than see.

III *Early Symbolism*

Although Green could quite early handle symbolism easily, he is in *Blindness* more direct and traditional than he is in his subsequent diversionary tactics and obliquity. The obvious symbolic structure is based on the two principal subjects of the novel, blindness and growth. Besides the literal process of adjusting to and overcoming physical blindness, the conditions of sight and blindness symbolize the farther-reaching aspects of maturation and growth. Sight indicates knowledge of the exterior world in which John Haye at first lives abundantly if immaturely. As his diary reveals, he is beginning to explore literature and life, but he is in the darkness of immaturity and self-centeredness.

When John is blinded, he is plunged into a literal darkness that is complicated by his immaturity. For a time, he considers Nanny, Mrs. Haye, the nurse, and other people around him as simply helpers or entertainers who should leave him alone when they become tiresome. Since his character John must grow from within himself into the interior light of self-knowledge and maturity, Green unfolds the long and complicated process carefully and sensitively. John develops an understanding of Joan, her problems and character, and their true relationship. Then he forges a future for himself which, as far as he can see, is the best he can do: not vegetating in the country but working under the vital influence of the city. He believes so strongly in his solution that he sacrifices his stepmother and their estate for it. His belief is shown to be true in the last forceful scene in which, engulfed by the sound of bells, he overcomes the last great obstacle to his maturity and adjustment. He demonstrates his success by writing to an old friend (as he had not since his accident) and thereby reestablishing connection with the external world.

Another type of symbol in *Blindness* occurs toward the end when John and his stepmother are passed on their way to the train by a speeding motorcyclist. If, as John Russell has stated, the speeding

boy epitomizes the undirected, impatient rushing of youth, then the
scene with the motorbike symbolizes "the entire psychological di-
lemma of John Haye," who was rushing to London and who was
dreaming of a crack express train which would stop for no one else (it
turned out to be a local).[7] The motorcyclist fits William York Tindall's
term "epitomizing symbol" and is as straightforward as the structure
of *Blindness*. The young Green may merely have intended the
youthful speeder as a contrast to John, for he cannot speed, but must
allow others to do it for him, and he is always being slowed down—
something else he must accept.

IV *Narrative Techniques*

Green at twenty demonstrates narrative skill not usually attained
until after much reading, thought, and experimentation. His sure,
artistic approach to the novel is evident in several techniques which
developed throughout his canon and in a few satisfactory techniques
which he did not continue. In *Blindness*, he divides the plot into
three parts which at first glance do not seem unified. Part I is
selections from John Haye's diary during his last year at Noat School.
Part II relates his first months of blindness but devotes a large section
to Joan Entwhistle. Part III portrays his growth toward adjustment
and maturity. After each part is a letter; the first two serve as
transitions and summaries; the last, as summary and resolution.

Besides a steadily chronological progress of the action, the major
unifying factor is the theme, which is supported by the titles of the
three parts, "Caterpillar," "Chrysalis," and "Butterfly" that signify
growth and organic development. The caterpillar is an immature
John Haye who lacks not only self-knowledge but also sympathy for
others. The chrysalis is a cocoon of darkness in which changes occur
slowly and imperceptibly, and the butterfly suddenly bursts forth
fully grown in a kind of glory which John himself experienced.
Ultimately, this approach is a direct and not an oblique one; but, in its
seeming indirection, the plot of *Blindness* hints at the "nonrepresentational" concepts Green expounds later.

Another element of narrative technique is description and its basic
role in creating a setting. Again, Green gives more and richer detail
than in his later novels. His settings are appropriate, for example, to
John's blindness and to Entwhistle's depravity. Always, even in the
city, the descriptions include natural elements like flowers, birds,
sun, and weather. Green, who concentrates often upon minutiae,
brings the tiniest details of the setting to our attention as if they are

important; and they are, though not as a microcosm that reveals a macrocosm. Rather, they take on an importance for themselves, especially to the blind John or to the materially deprived Joan. In the following quotation Green builds his description, tracing John's consciousness, from the most trivial to the immense: "The evening was falling away and the breeze had dropped. A midge bit him on the ankle and a drop of sweat tickled him by the bandages. The pigeons were all cooing together, there seemed to be no question and answer. . . . Birds twittered happily and senselessly all round. Through it and over it all there was the evening calm, the wet heavy air everywhere. The sky would be in great form. . ."(92). He also begins alternating blocks of dialogue with blocks of description, a process in which dialogue increases through the total canon until description virtually disappears in *Nothing* and *Doting*.

V *Characterization*

The greatest accomplishment and complexity in *Blindness* is Green's characterization. At least the four major characters—John, Mrs. Haye, Joan, and Mr. Entwhistle—are fully realized and are imaginatively rendered individuals who, with the exception of John before his tragedy, are not created wholly from Green's own experience. Besides the solid middle class, the picture of normality, he deals with declassed and abnormal characters. Green began developing his characters mostly by dialogue and scene, with a limited amount of outright description and commentary, but the most impressive aspect of this first novel is his use of revealing parallels and oppositions which comprise the character's interrelationships. Whether intentional or not, Green establishes roles for his male and female characters that presage situations in later novels. As noted previously, the female characters tend to be stronger than the male; or the male characters, at least for a time, abandon dominant roles to the female. According to Russell's theory, the males in Green's novels are often static while the females are so dynamic that they cause a fundamental opposition. Mrs. Haye and Joan maintain strength and responsibility because they remain active, but John and Mr. Entwhistle suffer defeat because they are inactive. Green usually provides a solution for his characters, however unsatisfactory it may be, as long as they can act. In the long run, only Mr. Entwhistle is completely defeated because all action is frustrated. The parallels are given variety: a mother cares for her son on the one side and a daughter for her father on the other. By means of these oppositions and parallels, conflict is created and enabled to work toward a resolution.

Dialogue is effective through the accurate reproduction of speech patterns that range from those of the middle to the lower class. Green, as omniscient author, varies the tone and style with each character who speaks, not only aloud but also to himself. The contrasts between what the characters think and what they say reveal their personalities uncommonly well. Typical is the cordial conversation of Mrs. Haye, John, Nanny, and the nurse. When the nurse hints at leaving, all are polite but have different interior comments. Mrs. Haye: "Thank God, the woman was talkin' about goin'." Nanny: "Time she went, too, airified body." John: "The nurse was intolerable, but at least she was alive, and now they were sending her away" (91).

John Haye especially, since he is the central figure of the novel, is well characterized by what he says. His growth process is traced by his speech, but, because of its personal nature, such growth involves interior as well as exterior comments. However, his thoughts are not reproduced with the complexity of a fully developed interior monologue. Monologues by necessity, they are the novelist's selected ideas, oriented toward what they must reveal about the character, not the character's stream of thoughts containing a seemingly confused free association. Green has said that "there's no 'stream of consciousness' in any of my books that I can remember—I did not read *Ulysses* until *Living* was finished."[8] Impressively portraying the blind person's point of view, Green causes John to think about his situation often and to draw inward. When John talks about some of his problems with Joan, he is more self-revelatory to her than to anyone else.

John's growth pattern is easily traced through three stages that correspond with the three divisions of the novel. In his diary, an immature schoolboy verges on being a dilettante. He is sensitive to beauty in painting, music, and literature; he is exploring his world; and many of his reactions are typical ones. He is amused at the provinciality of his home village and has religious doubts; he belongs to the clique that creates disturbances at political campaigns and in summer military camps; and he frequently shows self-understanding as when, during his social ostracism, he admits being difficult to get along with lately. Moreover, John's streak of unsympathetic action makes him party to minor schoolboy pranks upon and threats to those on the fringe of his group. Near the end of his diary, however, John is beginning to seek his own way while refusing a bid for the Essay Society, for example, and while looking more toward his projected literary future. On the whole, his character is normal; it is immature but has signs of both strength and sensitivity.

After his accident, John begins the long, difficult maturation process, but one that is more complicated than usual. The test of his inner strength is a gradual process that involves pain, then self-pity, and later attempts at self-discovery. Even during the lonely early period of his blindness, John Haye admits truths about himself which point the way to enlightenment. He begins to tire of the nurse, his stepmother, and Nanny. Once when the nurse is preparing his bed, he sits on a chair and feels the throbbing head pains. "And this atmosphere of women," he thinks. "There was no male friend who would come to stay, he had always been too unpleasant, or had always tried to be clever, or in the movement. And now there was no escape, none" (95). Though he feels stifled by so many women, his first reaction is to regret the death of his real mother and to speculate about whether or not her presence would have eased his difficulties. Next he drifts with the current and allows his stepmother to arrange his life and to include him as best she can into her rural existence at Barwood. This attempt to shift his burdens to another, as John Russell has noted, forms a pattern found in other novels such as *Caught* and *Back*, but it appears for a time in *Blindness* to be more literal than figurative or symbolic.[9] Finally, John constructs an idealized relationship with Joan to relieve his loneliness.

Beginning to feel a tentative adolescent love, John learns more about himself and about life by talking with Joan about much of his confusion. At first he speaks more at the girl than with her while she, in her deprivation, only partly understands. Gradually, they come to understand each other as they discover themselves. Realizing that neither can ever be part of the other's world and that each wants to grapple with what each considers to be his own life, they separate. John recognizes that his imagination has been partly responsible for their relationship; and he calls her Joan, instead of June, when they part, signifying his acceptance of reality (205). When he finally asserts himself, he regains his literary ambitions, convinces Mrs. Haye that they should sell Barwood and move to London, and bids Joan farewell. London, at first, is more confusion and frustration, including an attempt to flirt with his landlady; but in a flash as physical as it is spiritual, he eventually passes the point of doubt and gains self-possession. After the bells and the "fit," he hears the traffic not as chaos but as "busy vibrations" (254).

Mrs. Haye, John's stepmother, is a caretaker figure. She is a strong women, horsey, unsentimental, practical, and provincial—just the type to take responsibility for a blind son if she can also control him. Her strength, however, is her weakness; for she is unable to function assertively except on her own terms and in her own milieu. Green knew the type from astute observation of women he knew and was able to reconstruct such a personality. Her landed-gentry attitude toward the dependent village of Barwood, organizing and managing it, was her entire *raison d'être*. Lacking John's sensitivity and his artistic interests, she is baffled in her attempts to help him, not knowing that John can succeed only when she fails; for John must never vegetate in the country with no more creative outlet than conducting a workman's literary society. Her regrets at his never being able to ride or hunt, her plots to marry him off as best she can, and her inability to discuss literature with him are normal traits. But ultimately, though she is one of Green's active, dynamic women, Mrs. Haye must be overcome and condemned to a static existence in London so that John can lead his own active life.

John has, therefore, the added complication of coping with both women if he is to be freed from his isolation; but Mr. Entwhistle, who has only his daughter for company, is drawn deeper into isolation. Young Green's creation of the Entwhistles is impressive not only technically but also creatively, for such an abnormal situation was beyond his immediate experience. However, Green needed the situation for plot resolution; for Joan is important for both her opposition and her resemblance to other characters. She is stolid and unimaginative about the natural beauties which thrill John; she is uneducated and unread, but John is not. Nonetheless, she, like John, has entered a sort of darkness, for, having been forced away from the cleanliness and color of the vicarage, hers is a squalid life of sensation rather than of intellect. Her daydreams involve a young farmer, and her enjoyment of her surroundings comes from the weedgrown decay of her neglected house and garden. Joan reacts normally enough to John's flights of fancy and to his delicate motions toward flirtation; but they are really too subtle for her. She betrays a psychological abnormality, however, in her almost masochistic feeling about male violence: she likes young George because he is rough, and she trembles with a perverse sort of pleasure when her drunken father staggers to her door and is disappointed when he does not try to force it open. Like John, she has a scarred face; but the cause of it was her father's violence. If Joan were to gain much influence over John, it would have been abnormal rather than normal, for he would have been as stifled by her as by his stepmother's more normal influence. Joan's chief roles in the novel are to assist in John's growth into maturity and independence and to represent the opposite extreme—dulled insensitivity. Seeing how Joan is trapped by her father in a deprived environment, John vows rebellion against his stepmother to save himself.

Mr. Entwhistle also represents the opposite extreme of John's potential situation. The alcoholic, unfrocked clergyman has long suffered a figurative blindness which allowed his being made a cuckold when his wife was alive. Compensations, instead of leading him to constructive action and self-knowledge, merely force him deeper into blindness and self-delusion. He at first finds solace in growing roses; but, lacking self-control, he attends to nothing but his roses; for he wastes money, neglects family and church, and turns to alcohol, again with immoderation. After he is unfrocked, he sinks even deeper; he is caught, the reader feels, in an insoluble tangle of delusions of grandeur (his supposed genius) and of pain (his imagined cancer). Joan, by remaining active and by taking the responsibility of her father, still has a chance of salvation; but she gradually assumes some of his depravity. The reasons she gives for parting from John are her father's self-delusions: he is a genius; he is writing a great book; he will soon regain his lost position in life: and, more than that, he needs her, and she can control him. John has grown beyond her, she senses; and he soon will not need her care.

VI *In the Mood*

The general attitude of Henry Green's critics has been that *Blindness* is more immature than it actually is and that, after publishing it, he began a gradual development of his own seriocomic novel style. This attitude persisted even after Green published an article revealing that he had begun another novel, to be called "Mood," in the late 1920s and that he had never finished it. Edward Garnett, who encouraged him to finish "Mood" and to polish it later, evidently felt that the novel had possibilities. Its significance to us is that this novel, while showing some development toward the later novelistic style, was more similar to *Blindness* and to older novelistic traditions. Stylistic and thematic development of Green's novelistic art did not occur, therefore, after *Blindness* and immediately lead to *Living*.

"Mood" concerns a young lady with whom Green fancied himself in love at the time, and he planned to tell the story through her eyes. The heroine, Constance Ightam (pronounced "Eyetam"), and her good friend, Celia, drift apart after Celia's marriage; and this separation was evidently to be the principal conflict. Green showed little imaginative invention in his characterizations since the Ightam family could easily have been taken from people he had known. The Ightams have a country house in the Queen Anne style and a London house by Robert Adam, and Mr. Ightam naturally works in the city and spends weekends at the country house.

The interest of the novel and an indication of Green's potential development are in symbolism and psychology. Green chose his symbols, he reports, with deliberation; and they were evidently more obvious ones than those he would use later. Kings and queens are his private symbols of his love for the original of Constance (though it appears that he remains only the narrator and does not make himself a character in the novel). Evidently the symbolism is somewhat Freudian because Green mentions pointedly that Professor Freud was still living when "Mood" was being written. In any case, each character has his personal symbol, one which Green calls "the love for a significant object." Constance, for example, keeps as her symbols "two small bright painted aeroplanes in wood" on her mantel;[10] and these objects can be construed as sexual symbols when she notices that they no longer look like kings but like queens. She must be a bright, vivacious modern girl who also has some feeling for the past because on the same mantel are Delft candlesticks and an Old Dutch clock.

Even as a young author, however, Green had the esthetic judgment not to finish the novel. He felt that the situation was too static and that the characters were not animate, and this inertness told him that he could not finish the novel. The final reason for quitting once again supports a personal motivation for his writing novels, for his love for the original of Constance died about a week before he wrote the last words he could on the novel. "And that, perhaps," he writes, "is the whole explanation."[11]

After his retreat from "Mood", Green began to develop his novelistic techniques in the direction they were to go. In spite of some technical similarities, *Blindness* and *Living* are as different as an

English public school and an English factory. Of all the things that Green might have done in his youth, his work in the Birmingham foundry proved most fruitful; for his experiences were the turning point in his writing career that his completion of "Mood" could never have been.

CHAPTER 4

Work and Play

IN *Living* (1929), Green turned more clearly toward a narrative style and technique which he continued to develop in his other novels. More than in *Blindness*, he also used the themes found in his later novels; for he fictionalized his personal experiences which motivated him to write each work. Before writing *Living*, Green has recorded in *Pack My Bag*, he had begun to feel the stirrings of social conscience and to doubt "whether there should be great inequalities between incomes." This feeling caused him to leave Oxford and go "to work in a factory with [his] wet podgy hands" (195); and *Living* was the result of this labor experience. It was as if Green were living for the first time, and his novel evokes such a feeling. The subject is not himself, however, but the new class of people he met. Instead of writing a sociological treatise or a documentary novel, he wrote about real individuals who are caught by the limited means of their social class but who do somehow live. The working class, he learned, talks about people without pseudointellectual pretense but with consuming interest in the fundamental activities of living. Moreover, his experiences gave Green reliable knowledge of different classes which helped him portray characters throughout the social spectrum.

The writer, then twenty-four, achieved only moderate success with *Living* because of rather mixed reviews; but it aroused the enthusiasm of contemporary writers like Evelyn Waugh, Stephen Spender, and John Lehmann. To them *Living* remained, until after World War II, an undiscovered masterpiece among proletarian novels. More recently, it has been praised as "the best English novel of factory life, though," as Walter Allen says, "to put it in such terms, is almost inevitably to see it wrong, as it was for years."[1] Green was not a sociological novelist or one of the young Communist-oriented writers of the 1930s, and his novel was not so much a study of factory life as of the people whose work was, one way or another, factory work. Some scenes inevitably are set in the factory, but many others

44

are in the characters' homes, in streets, or in other places where such people have what fun they can. The workers do not strike or recount tales of dire oppression, and the complaints by workers about employers or by employers about employees are not the expected ones. The inspector stationed at the washroom door to prevent loafing, for instance, is discussed by the workers with greater concern and indignation than are their unsafe working conditions.

The major complaint contemporary reviewers made about *Living* was that its style contained "crude affectations" and "footling little tricks" which obscured its genuine qualities.[2] The structure, too, with its short scenes and sudden shifts was criticized as inorganic. No one, however, adversely criticized the subject matter involving characters, actions, and universal themes; and no one expressed serious doubts about *Living* as a successful proletarian novel. An early reviewer described it as realistic; but, while Green's settings and situations are impressive in their verisimilitude, several later critics qualify the label of realism.

Green enriches the otherwise commonplace background of his action by stylistic innovations and by poetic and symbolic techniques which at times are beautiful if not fantastic. The subject matter, too, concerns more than factory life and working-class problems; for characters of both upper and lower social classes parallel each other in such a way that relationships as well as differences are shown. Workers' lives are contrasted with the managerial class to show that the workers are often deliberate and capable but are at the mercy of confused, at times inadequate, managers, who are most interested in self-betterment. The main plot, however, concerns the working-class couple, Lily and Bert; and their love affair is tragicomically concluded when Bert runs away in mid-elopement. Paralleling this situation is the love of the factory-owner's son, Richard Dupret, for the socially prominent Hannah Glossop, who rejects him. Burying his sorrow in work, Richard meddles with the factory, ruins his workers' careers, and damages the firm. The novel ends in failure for the elderly, like Mr. Craigan, but with some hope for future success by the young, like Richard and Lily. In fact, Edward Stokes summarizes the true nature of *Living* by calling it "a very satisfactory compromise between the social documentary and the novel of personal relations."[3]

I *Themes*

In *Living*, both parts of Stoke's "compromise between the social documentary and the novel of personal relations" contribute to the

major themes which Green uses with increasing frequency in later
novels. Personal relationships, for instance, carry the interrelated
themes of man's loneliness and man's search for love and happiness.
Green's characters are strikingly individual; each is a separate being,
not part of the mass, from Mr. Craigan in his attempt to maintain a
family not really his to Mr. Tupe in his toadying attempt to form a
relationship with Mr. Bridges, the manager. The resultant theme of
loneliness is emphasized by the novel's epigraph which is not the
expected Classical quotation but a key line in the novel itself. When
the pregnant Mrs. Eames asks herself the question, "As these birds
would go where so where would this child go?" (246), she refers to the
circling pigeons that symbolize the desire to escape from and the
longing for home; but the immediate context links them with the
miracle of birth which so befuddled Mrs. Eames. By logical extension, her question is that of every person who must seek alone the
meaning of life.

Man's loneliness in this novel is interrelated with his search for love
and happiness as he seeks happiness through love and sometimes in
marriage. Both Bert Jones and Jim Dale unsuccessfully seek a
marriage with Lily Gates, who is also seeking marriage. Richard
Dupret is in love with Hannah Glossop, who loves Tom Tyler, but
these loves, too, are unsuccessful. Only Mr. Craigan finds success in
his attempt to keep Lily, whom he loves like a granddaughter, in his
home; but their relationship is unsatisfactory and probably temporary. Green tempers, as usual, the unhappy outcome by having most
of the characters retain some future hope.

As for the "social documentary" aspect of *Living*, the situation at
Dupret's foundry is similar to that at the time of the General Strike;
but the novel is not truly historical. Green's continuing theme of
social dissolution is developed mainly by the opposition between the
younger and the older generations. The elder Dupret runs his
foundry in a more personal manner than his son, who considers his
father's system old-fashioned; but Richard substitutes only his inex-
perience and self-centeredness. Indiscriminately firing older men
and retaining younger men, who are less efficient because of their
struggles for position, Richard effects the breakdown of industrial
relationships. Social and industrial problems are inevitable because
older workmen are cast adrift with little or no pension and younger
laborers find themselves increasingly dissatisfied.

II *A Telegraphic Style*

In *Living*, Green first establishes most of the elements of his technique and style not found in *Blindness*. Where his first novel possesses a richer, more descriptive style, his second is more austere and compressed. Although both stress dialogue and include much rich description, *Living* contains noticeably less description than *Blindness*. Moreover, Green's attempt to remain neutral as a novelist begins with *Living*, where he avoids imposing his own views on the action by providing less description and more accurate dialogue. In addition, as he stated, Green believed that his elliptical or telegraphic style would reproduce the atmosphere of factory and laboring life in which he himself was then involved. He also uses figures, as one would probably do on a factory report, instead of spelling out numbers. His sentences are mostly short, and his punctuation is simplified. Although he is not trying to shock his reader, the prose in *Living* admittedly does demand some initial adjustment by the reader.

The elliptical style of *Living* achieves tautness and compression, but the novel is not austere and arid. Though most of the action takes place in the grimy foundries and in the colorless streets and houses of Birmingham's laboring section, the setting is not allowed to remain drab but is given lively and colorful poetic imagery. Green uses elaborate yet restrained descriptive passages full of motifs, metaphors, and symbols; and he emphasizes his characters' tendency to speak of colorful objects.

Almost in the manner of E. M. Forster's novelistic uses of recurring items, Green weaves into his story objects, actions, and phrases which often enhance theme and characterization and enrich setting. Though not with the regular consistency of motifs in, for instance, Forster's *Howard's End*, the motifs of *Living* convey the feeling that the characters are alive and that their struggles for independence and security are truly realistic living. In this story of a northern industrial city, Green avoids a cold, monochromic effect by means of warm, colorful, tropical motifs. Through rich tropical landscapes, Green thereby avoids the drabness of reality and also emphasizes a major theme—the desire to escape and to assert independence while longing simultaneously for home and security. In their imaginations, young characters practically live in the tropics, where life seems so much easier than their own. Early in the novel old Mr. Bridges, the foundry manager, uses distant Siam as a codeword for financial disaster; but later young Tom Tyler returns from the real, exotic Siam and wins Miss Glossop's heart. Miss Glossop's emotions invest daydreams of tropical oceans, islands, flying fish, and birds with the consistency of personal symbols.

Lily Gates and Bert Jones attend movies set in the tropics and, for a time, plan to emigrate to a tea plantation. Lily's catch phrase is "H.O.T. warm" (27, 167), though with Bert her phrase expresses a sensuous mood while with Jim Dale her flippant use of the phrase shows her lack of interest in him. She also sees a black man in the streets (128), an event which she recalls (160) and finally construes as an ill omen when, on her elopement trip, she sees another black man wearing a green scarf (243). Lily, after her disastrous elopement, is compared to one cruising "across that well charted ocean towards that land from which birds landed on her decks" (255). Voyages that are frequently discussed in the novel range from Mr. Herbert Tomson's realistic plans for emigration to "Orstrylia" (12) to Lily's romantic dreams of sailing to Canada where the "golden light [covers] a golden land" (189).

Old Mr. Craigan is partially characterized by reading Dickens and by listening to the wireless. He reads little besides the novels of Dickens, and he continually rereads them. This preoccupation impresses Lily, who first comments on Mr. Craigan's reading habits. She does not understand his reading the same books again and again but concludes that "e's like the deep sea" (55). The old laborer comes closer than any other character in *Living* to being "deep" or introspective, but his reading habits reflect more of his character than this aspect. Craigan often recalls the past, the period of Dickens, who represents a concept of home and security; he establishes a home and family along patriarchal Dickensian lines, though he is not married. The only Dickens work mentioned by name is *Little Dorrit*, the novel of debtors' prison and one in which the working class is contrasted with both upper-class glitter and gloom. Feelings of helplessness and imprisonment pervade *Little Dorrit* and, when extended, add a dimension to situations in *Living*: Lily feels imprisoned and tries to elope; old Mr. Craigan grows helpless in forced retirement; and both Dickens and Green contrast in these novels the working class and the wealthy. Typically, Green makes no overt point about Mr. Craigan's interest in Dickens's fiction beyond giving the reader an interesting detail of the old man's life and reflecting sometimes Mr. Craigan's feelings. More may be implied about being trapped by unbearable circumstances for the rest of one's life, as in Evelyn Waugh's *Handful of Dust*, when Tony Last is doomed to a lifetime of reading Dickens to his captor, Mr. Todd. When Lily elopes, Mr. Craigan picks up *Little Dorrit* (also the last title mentioned in *A Handful of Dust*), but he knows he cannot read (222).

Green also enriches his style with "poetry of incident," Walter Allen's term in *The Modern Novel* for making an essentially realistic subject seem almost poetic: for instance, he cites the scene in *Living* in which Arthur Jones sings all day in the iron foundry. He does not sing often, but this time he sings in Welsh, "his silver voice yelling like bells" (90). No one else sang that day, but everyone stopped by the machine shop to hear him. Green, who evolves the mood with restrained economy, ends the episode with the reason for Arthur Jones's day of song: "That night son had been born to him." Uniting the biblical and telegraphic elements of his style, Green lends great dignity to the Welsh laborer and also dramatizes a supreme concern in the novel, the desire for children.

Birds and other manifestations of nature appear in simple images and in literal descriptive phrases. In *Living*, when the children go in to eat, the streets are left empty; and Green, needing a swift and evocative description, writes that there "were only sparrows now in streets" (108). The wings of sparrows, blackbirds, woodcocks, doves, gulls, and pigeons beat in the descriptions and in the characters' speech. Mr. Bridges in particular says ambitious people act like "crows after sheep's eyes" (11) and are hypocritically "cooing like a dove" (145). Such colorful speech helps to enliven and make expressive a rather drab managerial type and to encourage sympathy for his ultimately pathetic situation. All such references to natural manifestations prevent the novel's urban setting from becoming stylistically too starkly industrial and manmade.

After attempting in "Mood" to supply each major character with a personal symbol, Green achieves in *Living* a complex but discoverable success. Hannah Glossop's tropical daydreams of a more passionate life and Mrs. Eames's rescue of the sparrow caught in the window, as only the epitome of motherhood could do (19–20), are minor instances. Lily Gates, the main character, has powerful enough obsessions to assimilate objects and experiences to herself.[4] The principal objects that she assimilates with her obsessions are pigeons, symbolic of escape and freedom as well as of home and security, for Lily is obsessed with the threefold desire for marriage, children, and self-betterment. The first pigeons in this symbol system are kept by the man next door (13); but later, when Lily is preparing to elope with Bert Jones, she unconsciously identifies the pigeons with her own projected flight (199). After this the passages that apply become gradually more explicit, first, as a definite comparison with Lily's thoughts: "So, as pigeon when she had watched out of kitchen window had flown diagonally down in a wedge and then recovered themselves, as each one had clapped his wings and gone slowly away, so she drew back from him, her mind unbound . . ." (206).

Later, on the train, Lily's thoughts keep returning home in harmony with the pigeon's homing instincts: "For as racing pigeon fly in the sky, always they go round above house which provides for them or, if loosed at a distance from that house then fly straight there, so her thoughts would not point away long from house which had provided for her" (217). And after her ignominious return to Birmingham, the symbol is extended to include Mr. Craigan, whose destiny is now more than ever linked with hers (250, 251). As Giorgio Melchiori requires, this symbol does have a precise, consistent reference, but Green uses this personal-symbolic technique less often in his later novels.

III   *Techniques: Novel and Cinema*

The plot structure of *Living* appears to be more episodic than that of *Blindness*, but Green actually achieves more unity than is usually recognized because the novelist begins in this narrative the oblique approach which he brings into fuller play later. In addition, the novel's "structure and method are designed to illustrate . . . the inter-penetration of working lives and private lives and the inter-relationships between widely disparate social groups."[5] This "inter-relationship" stresses the unity of Green's plot, as it should, and shows how his sensitivity to pattern and form integrates plot and characterization.

The plot consists mostly of short scenes that shift rapidly from one character or group to another. Though the shifts are not necessarily in time, they frequently leap considerable space in order to bring the activities of a group of characters up to date and to keep the individuals animated. An especially skillful example occurs near the end of the novel when Lily and Bert elope to Liverpool. Interspersed with scenes of their travels are scenes back at Mr. Craigan's house showing the breakup of the remaining family group. The scenes are not disjointed or disconnected if viewed as a totality; but, as a contemporary reviewer stated, "the manner is cinematographic, a constant flicker of abruptly shifting scenes, a page or two in length, leaping from one group of characters to another."[6] The clue to the origins of this technique lies in its form and in the frequency with which characters attend the silent, flickering cinemas of that day.

Although this reviewer only claimed that the scenes were mechanically linked, we now recognize that Green connected his scenes through symbolism, through parallel or contrasting actions— especially between Lily and young Dupret—and with brief transitional devices. Unity is clearer, however, to the reader or the critic in retrospect than during the initial reading; nevertheless, the rapid scene shifts presage later development in Green's technique of presenting a block of description and then a block of dialogue. This technique in its turn led to the culmination of his novelistic theory that dialogue should convey both characterization and action and that description and authorial commentary should be limited to brief stage directions.

IV *Living Characters*

Green is more detached from his characters in *Living* than in *Blindness* and is objective, therefore, in his view of all social levels. He is working successfully with a larger cast, and he is utilizing dialogue and scene to individualize many of them, even several minor ones. Tarver, the ambitious draughtsman, for instance, is not only obsequious to young Richard Dupret, heir to the foundry, but is also continually demanding more assistants to produce fewer drawings. He is recognizable and memorable enough for a minor figure who is as inefficient and as much a "climber" as many young men are in his position. Although other members of the managerial and upper classes are drawn to life in the novel, Green achieves his best work in delineating his working-class characters. In spite of their drab lives and surroundings, the workmen and their women are more colorful than their betters. Green brings his characters brilliantly alive by weaving a web not of insinuations but of specific detail. His ear for realistic conversation is so accurate that Green does not omit the articles or employ striking sentence inversion in the dialogue as he does in straight narrative. Sentences such as, "Mr. Bridges went down through works in Birmingham till Tupe he found" (111) are not present in the characters' conversations. Though Green properly drops *h's* for his working people and for the managers who rose from the ranks, he achieves but does not exaggerate the lively and colorful language of a manufacturing city. His characters from the upper class speak more properly, but Green reproduces in their talk the languidness and boredom of the rich. The words of the ignorant, sycophantic workman Tupe are colorful if slangy: "God strike me 'andsome if 'e didn't raise 'is ugly old dial an' start blubberin' an' made such a 'ullabaloo as if 'e might be dead, or the only one in the shop" (111). The society hostess, while using figurative language herself, is more correct than colorful: "It was unfortunate I admit but don't see how she could have helped it. He had been no more alive than a log for months" (136). The speech of the characters reveals their personalities, even in minor cases, without much authorial description. This allows Green to remain objective and to stay out of his novel, as he intends.

With accurately colloquial dialogue, explicit narrative, and rich imagery and symbolism Green draws deep characterizations. The reader knows and reacts to the people in *Living* as individuals though they also represent their class. Green's interest noticeably is not in describing specific physical appearances or their ages. Jim Dale's face is strikingly handsome according to young Dupret, but the color of his eyes or hair is never specified. Lily Gates, whom Green describes only as plump, is clearly the main character, and her struggles to realize her desires are the ones the reader principally follows. By parallel, contrast, and extension, her problems are those of everyone else in the novel; and they are, therefore, more significant thematically than those of the upper-class characters. One critic declares that the young people in *Living* are adolescents; other readers may not consider them adolescent either chronologically or emotionally; for Green does not specify their ages.

Just as the novel is called *Living*, the problems in it concern living; and, despite the characters' continued efforts to live as they wish, most of them do not realize all of their ambitions. Some, in fact, are utterly frustrated. Lily's desires for marriage, self-betterment, and children of her own are repeated in variations throughout the novel and reach a sort of climax in her moment of mental anguish when she cries, "I, I am I"; says, "Why may I not have children, feed them with my milk"; and then prays for those things she most desires with a sincere poignancy not often found in Green's novels (109).

Mrs. Eames, her neighbor, provides both contrasts and parallels for Lily's situation as she suckles her firstborn, becomes pregnant again, and finally allows Lily to push the second baby in the pram.

From her meditation early in the novel as Mrs. Eames nurses her firstborn, she is the epitome of motherhood. When she asks, "Sons and daughters why do we bring them into the world?" her answer is a comfortable, "Because, because . . ." (24–25). Before expressing this thought, Mrs. Eames demonstrates her motherly capability when she is called to Mr. Craigan's house to rescue from between the upper and lower window frames a sparrow which none of the men could capture without harm, for Mrs. Eames reaches in quickly, cradles it gently, and releases it outside (19–20); she has the gentleness needed in such delicate operations. Lily, Mrs. Eames, the baby, and the pigeons on the novel's final page are enough to show the kinship of the two women in their natural desire for marriage, children, and self-betterment; but Green makes this connection even more explicit when he says that "Their relation one with the other was like 2 separate triangles" (246). They are separate, but their desires have the same shape.

Mr. Craigan is one of Green's old men who control those around them or seek comfort in the *status quo*. Mr. Craigan shelters Joe and Lily in his house so long that they become his family. Lily, who calls him "Grandad," loves and respects him rather than her father. Craigan in return loves Lily, but he controls her with a sort of benevolent despotism because in her lies his present and future comfort. When Mr. Craigan is discharged from the foundry and becomes ill, he feels his age, clinging to Lily more than ever. The role of caretaker shifts from him to Lily; but, as we observed, this responsibility does not make her any freer. Lily is active only by virtue of her ultimate role as a caretaker, and Mr. Craigan suffers ultimate defeat because he is unable to act.

Joe Gates is harmful to those around him as well as to himself because he is no longer his own man, having lost both his daughter and his position as the head of a family to Mr. Craigan. Even at the foundry, he is a satellite of the older man, though for a time he rebels by becoming friendly with Tupe, the manager's flunky and spy. Gates knows that he is offending Mr. Craigan, who despises Tupe; but, where Mr. Craigan is virtually alone except for his adopted family, Gates has no trouble finding cronies with whom to drink, gossip, and attend sports events. He is not thoroughly ineffectual, but he exercises his own kind of tyranny when he finds the opportunity. In the one violent scene of the novel, for instance, he strikes his daughter Lily, knowing that, in spite of Mr. Craigan's rebuke, Gates still has more of a right to lay a hand on her than anyone else.

When both old men have lost their jobs, Gates realizes that Mr. Craigan is his principal means of support; but he also discovers the hold he has over the older man. If Gates were to be evicted from the house, his daughter would have to accompany him because it would not be proper for her to remain alone with a man to whom she is not related. After playing this card, Gates also realizes that, if Lily were to marry and move away, he would certainly be forced out. His second villainous mission, then, is to prevent his daughter from marrying. He succeeds for a time, but Lily's desires as a caretaker are too strong. Green leaves his readers with the feeling that she will marry some day in spite of Mr. Craigan's well-meaning influence and Joe Gates's selfish machinations.

Not only does Mr. Craigan keep Lily near him, saying, "None o' the womenfolk go to work from the house I inhabit" (13). He also picks a husband for Lily. Jim Dale is another boarder in his house, so Mr. Craigan can expect, though not consciously, that Lily and Jim will remain with him. Jim, who is steady and dependable, is potentially a good husband; and, according to Dick Dupret and Mr. Tarver, he is also a handsome young man (3, 73). Dale, however, is moody and sober; and Lily does not want depression, she wants gaiety.

That Mr. Craigan's choice also happens to love her makes no difference. Love only makes him sulky; and, even during the movie in which a young lady loses her knickers in a full ballroom, he does not try to turn the situation to sexual advantage. Lily is titillated by the scene and calls Jim "you funny," but he is embarrassed. "Don't call me your names Lil when there's so many can 'ear you," he says (27). Green's characterization of Jim Dale is compact and subtle. In only a few direct scenes, Dale's conventionality is established; and, without showing any of his family background, his repressed upbringing is strongly implied.

When Lily elopes to Liverpool with Bert Jones, Dale leaves Mr. Craigan's house and takes a job at another foundry. Although he might return when Mr. Craigan sends Joe Gates for him, Gates couches his invitation in such terms that Dale sulks more than ever and refuses to return. Since the novel ends on an optimistic note for Lily, the cycle of Jim Dale's moods may return him to her. At least Green's portrayal of the character leaves that possibility open.

Jim Dale's moods make him seem like one of the more involved heroes of the silent movies and provide further references in *Living* to the cinema of the late 1920s. Besides the scene of Dale's embarrassment with Lily, there are other important episodes at the movies, especially with Lily and Bert Jones. Many of their ideas about life, love, and the future are acquired from the scenarios they watch. For instance, Lily's inspiration that she and Bert should emigrate to a tea plantation where, as we have noted, the weather is "H.O.T. warm." As his personal symbol, the lathe, shows Bert to be the inspired craftsman, so he derives romantic inspiration from the cinema; for instance, when he deserts Lily during their elopement to Liverpool. Equally important is the picture of Bert's family background that is made vivid not by the introduction of his parents but by the fact that they are nowhere to be found. Bert's increasing embarrassment matches Lily's increasing bewilderment as the couple search slums which become progressively worse until the forces of the pathetic and the comic in both their situations are intermingled.

Critics have noted that Green is unconventional in his treatment of Lily as the participant in an uncompleted elopment. The convention they have in mind is probably best illustrated by Maggie Tulliver in George Eliot's *The Mill on the Floss*. Where Maggie was ostracized, Lily was, to her almost equal discomfiture, ignored. After Mrs. Eames ascertains that no baby is coming as a result of Lily's adventure, she returns to her own family preoccupations. No one in the neighborhood is particularly interested, and Green characteristically makes no judgments.

Besides Lily Gates and related characters, the novel contains another chain of events involving Richard Dupret and his circle. Relationships in these cases, of course, refer to more than the families; and the two series of actions are linked, first, by the foundry where Lily's menfolk work and which Richard Dupret inherits. Also, as she is connected with Mrs. Eames in desires, she is connected with Richard in ambitions, at least for independence, marriage, and self-betterment; but both are frustrated and take unwise actions.

Though Richard is not the other self of Lily as Septimus Smith is of Clarissa Dalloway in Virginia Woolf's *Mrs. Dalloway*, the relationship is close in physical locations as well as in desires. In the cinema scene in which Lily and Bert Jones first become more than passing acquintances, Green develops a paean to moviegoers in "Europe and America, mass on mass . . . ," stating that "young Mr. Dupret was in a cinema" also (59). Thus Green stresses the cinematic pattern of the novel in the parallel situations. Later Lily and Dupret pass each other on the street unknowingly, but the author makes much of the occasion by emphasizing their parallel quests in life in spite of their differing social classes (188).

Once more the stasis of old age works for a time to inhibit the change which the younger generation in Green's novels often desires. In this case, old Mr. Dupret, by being a manufacturer of the old, paternalistic school, prevents his son from achieving independence coupled with wisdom and prevents his foundry from functioning smoothly without his direct control. Old Mr. Dupret, who is virile almost to the end of his life, is frequently unfaithful to his wife and is evidently reputed to have been more of a rake than he was. During his last illness, a famous harlot is sent for to warm his body, but he is too ill to say more than "goodnight." The illness itself is reminiscent of the early novels of Evelyn Waugh, for Dupret "slips on dog's mess" and injures himself (56).

Richard must compete with this father for his manhood, but he gives the impression of being neither virile nor emotionally mature. He surreptitiously picks his nose, a vulgar and childish habit which does not reflect creditably on his upbringing. An equally deft touch is Richard's comment about Jim Dale's beautiful face (3), for Mr. Bridges's startled surprise emphasizes doubt about the Dupret heir's virility and maturity.

The older managers such as Mr. Walters of the London office and Mr. Bridges of the foundry become father figures for Richard to rebel against. Whenever they make an authoritative statement about the business or become too familiar toward him, Richard reacts defensively. He begins to feel that the old guard is too inefficient and that their methods are outmoded. He is correct, at least regarding their treatment of labor; but the fact is that they run the company more and more since the senior Dupret is old and ill. Where Richard attempts to beat these father figures, he only partly succeeds; for Mr. Walters is too firmly entrenched to be eliminated easily. But, since Mr. Bridges has no protection, he is retired like Mr. Craigan and the other old workmen. Because Richard asserts himself over the older generation selfishly and ineptly, his victims are embittered; and, as we have observed, their younger replacements are inadequate.

Hannah Glossop, the object of Richard's unsuccessful love, is also childish; she weeps uncontrollably, for instance, when a chauffeur she does not even know is fatally injured at her family's country house. Though initially interested in Richard Dupret, she can utterly forget him when Tom Tyler returns from Siam and is the life of the party as Richard is not. There are some parallels between Tyler and Lily's Bert and between Richard and the equally inept lover, Jim Dale. Other parallels relate Lily and Hannah, and the similarities in imagery used to describe their loves aid in this accomplishment. Just as Lily has her tropical visions of tea plantations from the cinema and from black men on the streets, Hannah has emotions represented by tropical seas with flying fish that leap onto the ship, and by dolphins and tropical birds (167–68).

What the characters say and do and the parallels in which the groups of characters act out their basically similar problems convey the ideas in *Living*. Man seeks success, companionship, and love; and from these quests come the complications in the novel. Related is the pictured opposition of the socioeconomic classes: the higher class fulfills its responsibilities ineptly and selfishly; and the lower class that is still being victimized shows greater stamina in facing its problems. Thus, the working class dominates the novel; and, since the emphasis in *Living* is on the serious business of working-class life, Green's next logical step is a novel more concerned about the playing class, in *Party Going*.

CHAPTER 5

Pigeon and Albatross

THOUGH Green chose the wealthy, playboy class as the dominant group in his satiric novel *Party Going* (1939), the work is not all humor or frivolity. *Party Going* successfully continues the serious themes and the techniques established in *Living*, but it develops both elements and adds dimensions of its own. This third novel, which occupied Green throughout most of the 1930s, embodies much social behavior observed in his own class, which Evelyn Waugh dubbed as the "Bright Young Things." Among Green's party-goers is only one married couple, Robert and Claire Hignam; but without self-portrayal, Green offers firsthand, prophetic observations of the Hignams and their unmarried friends which he had begun in the Dupret-Glossop portions of *Living*. Moreover, *Party Going* logically follows *Living* as a stylistic development. The language is still spare, but it is not the telegraphic style that Green had used to emphasize the workingman's dominant role. Instead, he increases the interspersal of rich descriptions in passages that are sometimes almost, but not quite, purple; and these sections are almost a relief after the spare ones, despite poetic implications which many interpret as ambiguity or a "gathering web of insinuations."

Green worked on *Party Going* for about a decade before offering it for publication; for, as John Lehmann in *The Whispering Gallery* has noted, the small fame and financial success of *Living* had discouraged Green. Leonard and Virginia Woolf, influenced by his previous near-failure, hesitated in spite of Lehmann's enthusiasm before allowing the Hogarth Press to publish the novel in 1939. Perhaps Lehmann's tendency to include *Party Going* with *Living* as a proletarian novel represents the critical reaction to Green's third novel, both then and until recently. The proletarian feeling is present as a thematic thread but only by implication, for Green shifted his subject into the upper class and depicts the proletariat mostly through eyes befogged with wealth.

In this novel, some young friends start for a party in the south of France. Fogbound at the railway station, their money buys shelter in the station hotel, where they flirt until the fog lifts and they can resume the trip. Into their midst from the crowd of common people in the station are carried an ill, elderly relative of one party-goer and a dead pigeon wrapped in brown paper. The mysterious illness and the symbolic pigeon reveal the shallow lives of the young upper-class group but imply much more. The book, read only on the simplest level, conveys the frivolity and emptiness of the people; but, as some critics have observed, the novel's poetic elements imply more and convert the bare incident into "something rich and strange."[1]

The harshest criticism of *Party Going*—"a book fully as trivial, monotonous and meaningless as the people and the incident the author has undertaken to describe"[2]—came after the United States publication in 1951 rather than after the first British publication in 1939.

I *Themes:* Party Going *and* The Ancient Mariner

In the long view of *Party Going*, the characters and events are shallow and frivolous; but Green may be trying to tell the reader something rather than bore him. Major themes in *Party Going* clearly continue from the thematic concerns in *Living*; but, as Stokes admits, *Party Going* cannot be described in a single thematic statement. The major themes in *Party Going*, similar to those in *Living*, are man's loneliness, his search for love and happiness, and the dissolution of his social world. United, these three themes show the problem of man's finding his place in the order of existence and support Kingsley Weatherhead's assertion that in this novel, as in all other Green novels, the theme is self-creation.

The problem in *Party Going* is, however, that the individual's quests for place and order are not consciously realized or articulated. The characters, rather than creating, are seeking what is already created; they have already arrived, but they do not know it. An additional complication to the recognition of the theme in *Party Going* is, as critics frequently have asserted, that there is no central image, that the thematic threads remain apart, and that they are never completely interwoven. The problem with *Party Going* is that the seemingly dominant images and symbols, such as the railway station or the fog or terms related to death, are not dominant but merely contributory.

The most dominant image is, in spite of the critics' concerns about its mysterious ambiguity, the pairing of Miss Fellowes, the elderly relative who becomes ill, and the dead pigeon which, like Samuel Taylor Coleridge's Ancient Mariner and his albatross, she cannot relinquish of her own volition. Like *The Ancient Mariner*, *Party Going* can be read on several levels or, to be more explicit, can be read for several themes. The affinity of the novel for the poem is useful in clarifying Green's meaning, for such consideration discovers striking similarities, though there is no evidence that Green used Coleridge as a direct source.[3]

Characters reveal their loneliness in various ways: Miss Fellowes in her illness, Max and Amabel with their wealth, and the servants with their vigil over mounds of luggage. The theme is developed, as it is in *Living*, both by showing characters physically alone and by portraying their solitariness within a crowd. *Living* contains scenes of factory crowds, the press of humanity in a strange city, and the congestion of the wealthy at large parties; *Party Going* packs its wealthy characters into small hotel sitting rooms and the masses into a fogbound railway station. Especially when characters are alone in a crowd Green's theme is related to the spiritual isolation of *The Ancient Mariner*. One of the most congested scenes in which the main characters feel alone is set in the railway hotel lobby where several of the party observe vignettes like the one-eyed man who, after hesitating several times, struck a match for his cigar and ignited the whole box of matches. Coincidentally, Kingsley Weatherhead chooses this scene to point out a similarity with *The Ancient Mariner*.[4] Apprehensive people "standing in groups" create a naturalistic image like Coleridge's mariners who "listened and looked sideways up" (Pt. III, 1. 203). In the same scene, "almost every woman was having tea as if she owned the whole tray of it"; but she was alienated while crowded into the lobby (59).

The major upper-class characters retreat from one mass of humanity in the station to another in the hotel while holding their individual needs within themselves and while leaving the servants in the teeming station with whatever private thoughts they might have. Julia Wray, who especially represents her superior class, views the lobby and later the upstairs sitting rooms (with adjoining bedrooms) which Max Adey, the wealthy host, has engaged to protect his friends from the mob. Even there they cannot escape because, while seeking to pair off and allay their loneliness, they are crowded into the small rooms; and they often see through their windows the crowd in the station below. For example, Julia, to make conversation, shows concern about the sea of people below at one time; at another, she is relieved that the crowd cannot reach her while she is feeling happy when the Welsh athletic teams begin to sing (152). The masses are dehumanized to the point that we are reminded of the Ancient Mariner, who blesses the water snakes, but Julia's vacillations parody his sincere act. At the end, when the trains begin running again, Julia calls them "dear good English people" but only because they cause no trouble (249). Julia and her party do not feel for their fellow creatures so strongly as the Mariner nor do they realize what they lack.

Additional underscoring of the characters' loneliness is found in Green's use of the unspoken soliloquy that is delivered by rich Alex Alexander and that is as explicit thematically as Green ever gets. Alex feels alone while the others are bustling about him, but he also touches regretfully upon the changes occurring in the group:

It was all the fault of these girls. It had been such fun in old days when they had just gone and no one had minded what happened. They had been there to enjoy themselves and they had been friends but if you were girls and went on a party then it seemed to him you thought only of how you were doing, or how much it looked to others you were enjoying yourself, and worse than that of how much whoever might be with you could give you reasons for enjoying it. (195–96)

Alex is pinpointing the quest of his lonely friends—and himself—for love and happiness. Fulfillment is not forthcoming, however, because these rich, bored young people are unable to form natural relationships. Though the girls feel pressed into the chase for men, they are unable to find release in honest desire.

The fabulously rich Max Adey is, so Alex indicates, the girls' prime target. In the separate suite upstairs, Max chases Julia, who has gone there to be chased; but he cannot rouse her to real desire. She tells him to stop, that she'd rather not be mussed before they leave; but, to insure her wish, she grants him a kiss. Downstairs the uninvited Amabel arrives to join the party and the chase; and she lures Alex into the bedroom so that she can be properly appreciated as she bathes in the adjoining bathroom. The only deeply felt love that Green describes is "a crawling frenzy of love" that Robin Adams feels for Angela Crevy. Robin does not want her to go on the trip to which he is not invited, for he jealously fears that she too will join the chase for Max. Though Angela appreciates his enslavement to her, she plans to do just what Robin fears.

The third separable theme is the dissolution of the social structure, especially that of the upper class which finds itself as superfluous in its twentieth-century way as did the title character in Ivan Goncharov's *Oblomov* in nineteenth-century Russia. However, the loneliness and the inability to love spontaneously or deeply, which the wealthy youths of *Party Going* experience, signify much more than the problems of one social class; for Green develops, on an allegorical level, man's plight in the twentieth century. Probably Green did not know when he began *Party Going* early in the 1930s what he realized by the time he had published the novel in 1939—that the world was sliding inevitably into another widespread war and that he was creating a British version of Robert Sherwood's *Idiot's Delight*—for he demonstrated that the existing social structure could not continue without some sort of cataclysm.

While in *Living* what Lily Gates and Richard Dupret desired took similar shapes, in vitality and depth of feeling the proletariat was stronger. As Green reminisces in *Pack My Bag*, the wealthy become "constipated with things they cannot grasp" as a result of inventing things to fill their leisure. In the iron foundry, he recalls, lunch hours were spent discussing people and concrete things such as "where a certain Stony Lane had been, which, soon after the war, had been obliterated in a clearance scheme in the district" (238–39). His point is that the lower classes were retaining their sense of reality but that the moneyed classes were becoming vitiated.

Alex's soliloquy elucidates the theme of *Party Going*, for he emphasizes the differences between the people crowded together in the cold, damp station and his party safely established in three hotel suites, including a bedroom in which Miss Fellowes can be ill:

That is what it is to be rich, he thought, if you are held up, if you have to wait then you can do it after a bath in your dressing-gown and if you have to die then *not as any bird tumbling dead from its branch* down for foxes, light and stiff, but here in bed, here inside, with doctors to tell you it is all right and with relations to ask if it hurts. Again no standing, no being pressed together, no worry since it did not matter if one went or stayed, *no fellow feeling*. . . . (195, italics mine)

Alex, who is exceptionally perceptive, speaks, this once, for the author, because instead of discovering more of the "fellow feeling" that Green revealed in *Living*, the other characters of *Party Going* recognize and have less of it. Because they are becoming more isolated spiritually as well as physically, it is little wonder that critics like Richard Stokes see so much of T. S. Eliot's *The Waste Land* here; but more forceful in this respect are the death images such as "the pall of fog," the "vault of glass," and the "wreath . . . of . . . blood" which help to make the fogbound station into Eliot's "death's dream kingdom" of "The Hollow Men." These relationships are striking; but before a full interpretation of the images used is possible, the pigeon, which Miss Fellowes bears in one way or another throughout the novel, has to be considered.

Alex's phrase "not as any bird tumbling dead from its branch" stresses the pervasiveness of bird references in connection with death. Miss Fellowes's pigeon not only symbolizes spiritual isolation, like the Mariner's albatross, but also images the theme of social dissolution. The Coleridgean term "Life-in-Death" precisely describes these characters' existence. For example, Julia and Amabel are preoccupied with their fight for Max; the endless discussions of Embassy Richard's letter to the newspapers demonstrate the meaninglessness of even the group's most energetic activities; Miss Fellowes's mysterious illness is treated as an annoying inconvenience and as the potential wrecker of the youths' plans. These interests and preoccupations weave into a pattern of isolation, frigidity, and alienation, and, to save their world, the members of the party must recognize their plight and form deeper and more responsible relationships. Instead, they convince themselves that they are not needed there any longer, even by Miss Fellowes, and they go happily off to France without having learned anything about themselves or others.

II   *Stylistic and Technical Development*

Party Going drops the elliptical style of *Living* and presages the greater use of dialogue and the richer interspersed descriptions of Green's later novels. The only important and indeed noticeable use of telegraphic style comes at the beginning in a poetic emphasizing of rhythmic accent: "Fog was so dense, bird that had been disturbed went flat into a balustrade and slowly fell, dead, at her feet" (7).[5] Instead of repeating the ellipses of *Living*, however, Green develops his description more fully in language containing sufficient articles and adjectives. The railway station, the fog, and the people's actions are all shown clearly and realistically. What is missing, to give more suggestivity to the opening scenes, is the elucidation of the motive behind Miss Fellowes's actions—both her motive and the author's—

relative to the dead pigeon. Surface motive is given almost as an excuse: someone might step on the dead pigeon and cause a mess. The motives of the nannies and Angela and her boyfriend are given, but they only emphasize what is lacking. Although Green provides in this novel realistic dialogue and description, he transmutes his realistic story into something poetic by suggesting symbolic meaning and allegorical levels beyond the surface.

Green's ear for dialogue, which is as sharp here as in his other novels, helps him peg the speakers as to caste and something more—an implication of their plight. The wealthy young things show their sophistication, it is true; however, their talk also demonstrates not so much innocence as ignorance of the real problems of life. Their boredom reveals itself in their repetition of inanities; and their confused frustration causes babbling and disorganized conversations that are reminiscent of the uncommunicating characters in Anton Chekhov's *The Cherry Orchard*. When Green's youths fear the mob has broken into the hotel, theirs is a dialogue of the disassociated and the isolated: "Oh, but then they'll come up here and be dirty and violent. . . . They'll probably try and kiss us or something" (235).

In fact, the servants in *Party Going* evince more perspicacity and patience than their employers, for they echo the working people in *Living* and forecast the servants in *Loving*. To the servants, their job is foremost; but one of them would like his cup of tea on time or at least a kiss from a pretty girl. Thomson asks, "Will you give us a kiss darling?"; and she does (160). Thomson's problem, like his employer's, is sex; but his approach is as natural as his urge (203). In direct, often laconic phrases, the servants speak concretely of concrete things; and British critics compliment the accuracy of Green's reproduction of the servants' speech that began with *Party Going*.

The novel begins almost like a poem by establishing regular rhythms with emphases on *fog*, *bird*, *flat*, and *dead*. Thematically, the concept of death is to be important; for, though the characters appear to be alive, so much of the talk among these bored young residents of limbo is flat and dull that theirs is a life-in-death. Already voyagers becalmed and fogbound, Green's party-goers are waiting to begin their trip to France, which is not an important one except for its representation of their customary useless activities. The important voyage for *Party Going* begins when Miss Fellowes acquires her albatrosslike pigeon and enters a tunnel marked for departures; for she too becomes a voyager toward death (125). The other characters imagine themselves dead, as do Alex (37) and Julia (59). The pouting boyfriend Robin is related to a dead calm (118); and, before the dead calm, the crowd in the station is linked with the mist from the water (86). Intermittently, a mysterious character, whose accent and supposed occupation continuously change, is a Protean character who, with his connotations of sea god or spirit, reacts favorably to Miss Fellowes's illness and unfavorably when told she is better (84).

Birds, as usual with Green, are profuse and are found, among other times, when new characters appear without explanation inside the locked and shuttered hotel. Amabel's eyes are like hummingbirds (154), and Embassy Richard is given the death sign in a feathered context when Max says cryptically that, "If he was a bird, he would not last long" (64–65). Birds also supply some unified symbols which are contributory to the whole novel, those associated with Miss Fellowes and Miss Wray. When the pigeon falls dead at her feet, Miss Fellowes picks it up on an impulse, washes it in the lavatory (a baptismal ritual), and wraps it in brown paper. Her efforts to be rid of it when she begins to feel ill are unavailing; she is impelled to take it up again. Though she did not shoot the bird, she takes whiskey for her ailment because her father had said that "it was good for everyone after a hard day" of hunting (24). As a young hunter, she saw many dead birds; but this one, seen in the city, shocked her so that "it did seem only a pious thing to pick it up, though it was going to be a nuisance . . ." (25). Later she is carried into the hotel, where her parcel breaks open causing great consternation and confused discussion. Miss Fellowes and her pigeon represent, as we have noted, the disintegration of her social class; but this point is missed by the other characters, as is illustrated in the conversation between Evelyn and Claire, which Evelyn concludes by saying, "Anyway it is definitely not a thing to worry about" (212). And, while making sympathetic statements aloud, they proceed not to worry about "it" or Miss Fellowes.

What they pass off as some kind of "sexual fit" continues as Miss Fellowes takes a terrifying voyage of her own through nausea and delirium that is at times described with imagery of a sea storm. Her inner tempest gains significance following a calm reference to the crowds in the station from whom smoke rose "like November sun striking through mist rising off water" (86–87). During the rest of the novel, the pigeon remains in Miss Fellowes's suite; and Miss Fellowes continues to bear her pigeon for the ills of her society as did the Ancient Mariner his albatross; but she is both unknowing and unrecognized. The question of her recovery may be answered along with the question whether Miss Fellowes loves "both man and bird and beast." Statements late in the novel imply that she, like the younger generation, never truly does (211, 212, 214).

Like the significance of Miss Fellowes, Miss Julia Wray unifies symbols which are also central to thematic aims. Though they become her personal symbols, they expand, as symbols do, to supply myriad implications. Julia, who desires but denies sex, arranges for Max to chase her but then refuses him. Having won a round over the other women who are laying snares for Max, Julia is content to rest on her laurels. That she has sexual desires, however, is made manifest by two sets of symbols: her charms, the artificial; and her memories of thickets and birds, the natural. Her charms—the egg with elephants inside, the pistol, and the top—are sexual with the *double entendre* of magic and physical charms. These are linked literally with nature because she once buried them in a thicket of bamboos or artichokes (later compared to the crowd in the station [178]). At this point, she becomes confused in spite of her specific sexual desires; and normal life is frustrated. Julia's private but natural symbols are seagulls which fly through the bridge she crosses on her way to the station (19), and she remembers them again in direct relation to a past experience with Max (151). When she last thinks of the gulls, they become confused with doves (symbols of love) at a time when her hopes to snare Max are highest (161). Though she tries to tell Max about her charms in spite of his disinterest (111), she does not recognize her natural desires well enough to mention the birds.

III   *Unity of Plot, Characters, and Meaning*

The plot is unified by the fogbound situation which involves characters, time, and place. Time is controlled by the arrival of the characters at the railway station at the beginning and by their departure when the fog lifts at the end. Only a few hours elapse, but enough for the reader to discover the themes without following the characters to France. The incident which unifies symbols and action and triggers a chain of events is Miss Fellowes's arrival at the tunnel marked "Departures," where she acquires the dead pigeon.

Unity of place is imposed by the fog, by the projected trip, and by the characters who become trapped and isolated like mariners on a long sea voyage. The setting is well planned to provide isolation in a crowd, an atmosphere of entrapment and depression which contrib-

ute to theme and characterization. Surrounded by fog, the garish
hotel lobby and the drab rooms contain hints of mysterious meaning;
they even become sinister when the Protean hotel detective arrives.
Mysterious and sinister implications sometimes mask the novel's
comedy and satire except for scenes like Max's upstairs chase of Julia
or the servant's kiss from a passing girl.

Unity of action is less easily discerned because the characters group
and regroup. Green, who must show events in several hotel rooms as
well as in the station itself, employs a cinematographic method to
dissolve from one scene to another; he sometimes uses brief
flashbacks, but events usually occur in straight chronological order.
Green's motion-picture techniques do not flicker quite so rapidly as
they did in *Living*; for movie technology improved after the 1920s.

The large cast of characters causes problems of another type
besides unity of action. Too few characters appear with frequency or
duration enough to facilitate thorough characterization. Through
dialogue, imagery, and symbolism, however, Green successfully
individualizes those important enough to convey meaning, and he
shows us enough about them as the party-goers talk and jockey for
position. As a focus of symbolism, Miss Fellowes is central; but, as a
focus for the characters' aims, Max Adey becomes central. Julia and
Amabel are chief rivals in *Party Going* who represent reserve and
sensuality in their contests for Max. Though the imagery is sexual, for
example in Max's thoughts of Julia (176–77), Amabel's feelings, which
are as cool and casual as Julia's, are motivated by boredom and by the
urge to maintain appearances through competition. By direct contrasts, Green characterizes and differentiates his two major female
combatants.

Max Adey is a type whom Green knew in those days, one of the
young men so rich that, as he noted in *Pack My Bag*, they were
"languid with money" (206). This type insisted upon paying for
everything and upon giving lavish parties to which, if they as hosts
came at all, they would come late and indecisively as Max did. Much
of the novel's irony plays around Max, for he is pursued by all women
but is truly loved by none. More ironic is Green's emphasis upon
Max's paying for everything but, as in the case of his stereotyped
apartment décor, his actually having nothing of his own. Identical
wealth and apartment décor and little else in common beyond a
surface sexual attraction draw Amabel and Max together.

Claire, the niece of Miss Fellowes, and her husband, Robert
Hignam, are with the group because they have little else to do but

attend parties. Their aimlessness is epitomized, as it is for the others, by Embassy Richard, who is so called because of his attempts to crash embassy parties—a meaningless activity for those who are always invited to the highest social functions. Nevertheless, his party-crashing combats boredom and fits his life's pattern. The legend of his activities provides a conversation subject for the party-goers that is fully as banal as his actions. Embassy Richard's sudden appearance is a surprise both because the hotel is shuttered and because Green often provides a Mrs. Grundy character who is never seen. What should be more consistent with the tone of the novel and the habits of the partying class but that Embassy Richard accompanies the group to France upon whim and after a last-minute invitation from Max?

The playing class of *Party Going*, aimless and unsuccessful in its interaction, is in a state of dangerous dissolution as Miss Fellowes's prophetic presence goes unheeded. When the fog lifts, the group gambols on to its party holiday in France—and leaves Miss Fellowes to her fate and the servants to their tea. The outcome of the social situation thus exposed, whether Green was being consciously prophetic or not, is World War II and the sociopolitical changes that occurred before and after it.

CHAPTER 6

Morituri Te Salutamus

T HE eve of World War II found Green with three novels published; and, with the foreboding felt by many in those days, he
saw an untimely end to his life before other novels, which he believed
were in him, could be recorded. In the last few moments that were
definitely left to him, he began a record that was considered by many
critics an autobiography but that was once included by him with his
novels. *Pack My Bag* (1939), a book motivated by crisis, is also a
reflection of the morbidity of its times.[1] "That is my excuse," he
writes in the second paragraph, "that we who may not have time to
write anything else must do what we now can" (5). The critical
appraisals of the book were mixed; they were mostly about the
qualities expected in a work by Green, but the consensus was that
Green wrote *Pack My Bag* too hastily for it to be totally effective.[2] The
hope for the future of English literature which John Lehmann had felt
after reading *Living* and *Party Going* was not encouraged by *Pack My
Bag* either by its tone or by its total accomplishment. The value of this
autobiographical work, Green was to tell Terry Southern eighteen
years later, was not in its picture of himself but in that of the era. If the
book is to have continuing value, however, it must have it because of
the portrayal of both a man and a period.

The period leading up to World War II, going back to and before
World War I, is significant; and this period Green covers, more or
less, in *Pack My Bag*. Admittedly the last ten years before World War
II would be difficult for Green to appraise objectively, but their
importance is so great that omission lessens the book's impact.
Therefore, he attempts to circumvent this situation by recurring
references to the threatening war. He describes family and school
incidents with an impersonal nostalgia, poetic but not evocative; but
he ends a decade before the time of writing. Green does not fully
develop important matters, however, even in those periods of his
early life which would most interest his readers. Our desire to hear

more about his literary background, for instance, is whetted by his statement that in his school "we were allowed to form a society of arts."

At this point, he "determined to be a writer" and chose a *nom de plume*, "of all names Henry Michaelis" (163). Echoes of John Haye in *Blindness* are clear but nevertheless intriguing. Green makes little of his school contemporaries and companions at Eton, though many of them were to become distinguished in the literary world. John Lehmann, who was on this roster, lists many of the others in *The Whispering Gallery*: Cyril Connolly, Anthony Powell, Eric Blair (George Orwell), Harold Acton, Rupert Hart-Davis, Peter and Ian Fleming, Alan Pryce-Jones, and Freddie Ayer. Both characters and activities of these literati-to-be and their influences on Green's literary development would have been useful subjects for development.

I   *Thematic Preoccupations*

Because Green felt that his role in writing this book was as an observer of his time, the themes that he believed relevant for his novels are found in *Pack My Bag*. Development and exposition of themes are not accomplished, however, so much as their origins are discovered and traced. The isolation of man, even though part of the mass, is found in the pages of Green's growing up as he learns about others. As a schoolboy during World War I, for instance, he inadvertently tempts a convalescent soldier beyond his strength. A bicycle ride leaves the soldier dangerously exhausted, though he hides the fact and thus removes himself from human contact. What young Henry Green learned in this particular experience is universalized. "We grow up by sharing situations," he writes, "what we share of another person's increases us, and my memorial to all of them at that time in my heart now is my anguish remembered as I saw him stagger in disclosed, wondering whether perhaps it were not my fault" (67).

Related to this unanswered question and the theme generally is what John Russell calls the theme of discontentment that is articulated when Green used the sentence, "Questions unresolved stay in mind" (35). Though Green was relating this question specifically to an experience during sexual maturation, he very well could have applied it to the exhausted soldier, so terribly exposed yet so withdrawn, and to the question of his own guilt. Russell expands the idea to illustrate important literary techniques of Green's "which harass the reader because things remain unexplained."[3]

Though full of scenes and actions, the book reveals no extreme childhood traumas. Though memorable scenes are indelibly printed on Green, they are not scars. He was born to wealth and comfort; he experienced no important deprivation; but he learned, over the years, a great amount about mankind and its problems. We can only credit his powers of observation, which he cultivated early, and his innate sensitivity for this insight. One of the things he learned was an unspectacular but invaluable lesson about the fate of adolescents as they grow to adulthood; but neither situation is applicable to Green until after 1952: those who did well in school often were burned out later or were content to rest on past laurels "so that they were too happy to do more than relive their successes over again once they had left" (167). His observations also included evidence that man's life in the modern world is fraught with snares to his happiness and that man must hold his suffering isolated within himself. Perhaps a reaction against such knowledge led Green to break his own reserve and to articulate his fear, and that of his generation, that he would be killed in the next war (78).

Green also provides a glimpse into the background of his thematic search for love which involves man's attempts to break out of his isolation. He criticizes sex education since sex, the way to make contact, is motivated by physical urges, as well as by spiritual discontent; for sex is Green's key to man's problems of, and relief from, isolation. With great respect, he surveys the boy's growth from childhood when "sex was a dread mystery." "No story," he writes, "could be so dreadful, more full of agitated awe than sex" (47). From there he moves into adolescence, rejecting the traditional comic treatment because it is "a time . . . that is of all the phases men go through one of the most moving because it will not be dismissed, the most alive of all his experience except when, perhaps seven years later, he high dives into love" (116–17). Finally, Green recognizes the problems of adulthood as he asks, "Can it be true that people genuinely feel they were happiest at school or is it because they are so miserable grown up?" (47).

The sheer naturalness of sexual processes evidently fascinates Green because his discussion of sex taboos is as positive as his attitude toward sexual maturation. The British boarding school comes under examination in his statement that "bodies should be objects of curiosity and it is a comment on the way we were brought up that we should find them exciting because forbidden." However, he also adds that he "would not have it any other way. Sex is the great stimulus and

. . . a great mystery as well in those [boarding-school] days . . ."
(124). Not only does he dwell in this autobiography upon his own
school days, but he also reproduces many of the telling events in a
short story entitled "A Private School in 1914," published at about the
same time.[4] As if to show how he could use the material in *Pack My
Bag* for fictional purposes, he repeats several instances almost ver-
batim; in fact, he reproduces his sermon on Peter and Jesus which he
quotes in the book (27).

More to the present subject, he dwells on the criminal implications
schoolmasters attributed to students' desire for privacy; for no one,
Green writes, was allowed privacy or close friends because those in
charge obviously felt something sexual would occur. The story is also
about the innocence of the boys as to sex and about what they did and
did not learn about behavior and about the headmaster's idiosyn-
crasies. The story never transcends factual origins, but its accuracy
about British boarding schools and sex education is borne out by
other writers such as, for example, Roy Fuller in *The Ruined Boys*.

In *Pack My Bag*, Green adds other details about how the growing
boy learns of girls. From what he calls "a time for boys to wait up over
windows" (124) to the point in his school career when he states, "I
began to meet girls" (172), his references to the feminine gender
increase. In France, while writing *Blindness* and while living with a
French family, he is so attracted to one of the daughters that he writes
poetry to her. Other incidents, such as when the boy says his dancing
partner's hair smells good, used later in *Doting* (32), continue to
explore this major source of relief from isolation.

He also is aware in *Pack My Bag* that society is in a state of change
and that his social class is in the greatest danger of dissolution, of
giving way to the classes below it. His opening statement, "I was born
a mouthbreather with a silver spoon . . . ," implies knowledge of the
ills of his class and begins a guilty refrain that runs throughout the
book. When Green matures enough to recognize his guilt feelings, he
temporarily joins the laboring class. Underscoring the beginning of
his self-consciousness—revealed by his writing both in style and in
content—is the time, 1939–40; for the start of World War II was, to
him, a cataclysmic event which threatened to speed the social
changes already under way.

Green's shifting of loyalty from his native class was gradual. As he
utilizes memory in this literary creation, he explicitly mentions the
interest he and his college generation had in Marcel Proust and *À la*

Recherche du temps perdu. Giorgio Melchiori points out similarities in Proust and Green, and not the least of them is a middle-class genteel view rather than an aristocratic world view. From this point Green descends even farther by stating, "at my public school I had hated every other face for fear the owner was a lord, at the university I was to court the rich while doubting whether there should be great inequalities between incomes" (195). He describes the excessively wealthy with detached disapproval: "their money snobbery at the university, their languid unpunctuality even at their own dinner parties, and their boredom with art, music, and literature from sheer surfeit of leisure" (238–39). His own interest in writing, which he considered something as natural as the growth of his fingernails, is compared to the laboring-class habit of taking night classes to improve a man's trade (238). The conversation of workmen in the iron foundry, he says, is more intellectual in its attachment to real life than the talk of his wealthy friends.

II *Symbol and Leitmotif*

In *Pack My Bag* Green continues vivid, sometimes lush imagery; and he provides, instead of symbols, a single leitmotif. Frequently he reiterates the belief that he and many others will die in the developing war. "This feeling my generation had in [World War I], of death all about us, may well be exaggerated in my recollection by the feeling I have now I shall be killed in the next" (78). Critics call the tone created by this continual repetition one of morbidity or self-pity, but it is really a natural reaction that many experienced to the growing danger. Green, however, sounds a note of challenge, if not one of outright defiance.

Earlier Green would have exhausted his defiance, and have been left with the realization of the actuality of war that he was to observe and to accept. In *Party Going*, he had warned about what was to occur in society; and he had little reason to doubt that the developing belligerence was related to the circumstances he had portrayed. Since all he had left to do was reiterate the already half accomplished fact, he used various approaches, working his comments into most unexpected contexts. For example, his memories of nature study at school elicited this twist on the usual: "Again they let us cut laurel up to mix with water in jam jars and this let off fumes to gas any butterfly we caught. It was thought less cruel to use gas than to stick them on pins. Our difference is, now we are older, we may die both ways at one time" (32). In *Penguin New Writing* (1945), Walter Allen called *Pack My Bag* "a crisis book" that resounds with recurring warnings of death and destruction.

III   *Style in Haste*

Neither the pressures nor the apparent haste of writing, however, kept Green from his usual style. At times compact and spare and often poetically rich and evocative, his style in *Pack My Bag* continues to be fascinating. As cavalier about strict grammar as ever, he uses the colloquial pronoun-antecedent agreement as in "I am not proud of this any more than anyone is of their nails growing . . ." (238). Even his birds swoop and hover again in such a memorable double simile as "one's thoughts like pigeons circling down out of the sky back to their dovecot set down where the river, sweeping to the sea, makes another like the last those birds make coming out of the evening" (53).

Green's quotations of juvenile writing provide in his autobiography a stage-by-stage account of his stylistic development. The childhood sermon which he used in "A Private School in 1914" is quoted as his own written before age twelve; and, though it contains all the candor and directness of which he was capable later, he notes that his style is also different. After describing in one sentence how Peter denied Christ three times before the cock crew, the schoolboy Green concluded his sermon flatly, "Now Brethren to be frank I think that it did Peter a great deal of good for he was a very weak man" (27). A description he writes not very much later entitled "Barque" is still in the schoolboy stages of his stylistic development, but it shows some beginning of the telegraphic style and mentions birds: "I sail on the sea by wind which is in the sky and I am the most beautiful thing on the sea. Stiffly I go, am borne upon the waters, and when I am near land the white gulls wheel then settle in the plenty of my rigging" (164).

The balladlike repetition of nouns and phrases also makes its appearance in this early Green. A bit more precocious is the selection beginning, "They have gone to bed too early, there is no courtesy now in guests." He continues, "For as the woman may lie awake after the man has finished, so may we be sent to our rooms by the empty chairs" (164). The resulting simile bears an amusing resemblance to the encounter of the typist and the young man carbuncular in Eliot's *The Waste Land.* In these early pieces, Green provides much of the stylistic interest of *Pack My Bag* because, though he continues the same intriguing audacity in writing as before, he is obviously a man in a hurry.

IV   *Autobiography or Novel?*

Green allows himself more than his usual freedom in narrative, perhaps because he tells about his own life; but he digresses more easily and intersperses more commentary and speculation. In his commentary, at least, he differentiates between fiction and autobiography. Since Green is not particularly reticent about the parts of his life which he includes, he is so illuminative that anyone interested in modern writing should read the book. Nonetheless, the comments he made, or was led to make, in his interview with Terry Southern raises a troublesome question: does he actually regard *Pack My Bag* as a novel, or is he merely accepting the autobiographical classification to avoid the problem this book presents?

Although *Pack My Bag* and *Blindness* both have autobiographical elements, he creates in neither what he considers to be a totally accurate portrait. No one, he says, can know himself thoroughly; therefore, his real purpose is to mirror the time. His narrative is basically chronological, as in his novels; and he develops the plot with what Phyllis Bentley in *Some Observations on the Art of Narrative* calls "scene" and "summary." The occasions that he chooses to emphasize are described with his usual attention to minute details as, for instance, in his bicycle ride with the wounded Australian soldier. Otherwise, he merely summarizes events to show the usual tenor of his life from childhood to adolescence to young manhood. He omits the 1930s, the period portrayed in *Party Going*; but the leitmotif of the coming war determines the tone if not the subject of *Pack My Bag*.

Green did repeat some subjects found in *Blindness*, and some references to the period when he wrote it. He wrote part of that first novel in France where he was interested in a French girl who could have provided a model for Joan Entwhistle. References to *Living*, slighter than those to *Blindness* but still present, concern memories about the languid rich of his university days that bring him up even to *Party Going*, but the characters in *Party Going* are clearly older than university students. His uses in subsequent novels of the events recorded in *Pack My Bag* are not so numerous as he thought they would be. The major example is that party where the boy tells his dancing partner that her hair smells good.

The foregoing discussion of his narrative implies vagary or uncompletion, but this is not the case. Green recreates his world by dwelling on minutiae and by metamorphosing them into the solid and meaningful setting in which life is lived. The book, however, remains focused on a candid narration of true events, though with proper names omitted, and is not transmuted into novelistic fiction.

V *The Problem of Names*

In *Pack My Bag*, Green's problem is his mixing the objective distance from his characters, which he prefers, with the necessary subjectivity of an autobiography. When he discovers after eighty-seven pages that he must decide whether to mention real people by name, he discusses the problem of putting family and friends into a book by name and then continuing to live with them. Also, if the person is well known, the reader may have his own opinion; and the writer loses control of what he tries to communicate. Fictional names are possible, but the character may be recognizable through the events, or the writer may find himself writing fiction. Green decides in favor of using no names even though he admits that if such an omission "as it often does make a book look blind then that to my mind is no disadvantage" (88). It does make the book rather "blind," and the readers wish he had been willing to retain the names. That he did not decide at once to omit names is more evidence that he wrote the book hurriedly. Of one character who is well and quickly realized, Green writes, "Most things boil down to people, or at least most houses to those who live in them, so Forthampton [his childhood home] boils down to Poole, who did not live in but was gardener about the place for years" (5).

Green's mother is sharply delineated mostly through her eccentricities, such as her shooting mangel wurzels bowled across the lawn by a reluctant Poole or her inability to command her many dogs (7). The emphasis is mostly concentrated on Green as a boy; and, as John Russell remarks, in spite of his ability to gain objective distance from himself, Green is able to evoke his relatively uneventful life with a sensitivity that makes even the most usual emotional experiences meaningful. For example, the French girl he met while writing *Blindness* is described, but she is always seen in terms of Green's attitude toward her. Her reaction to the poetry he wrote to her, however, is omitted so that he might express the Frenchness of her family, who thought his writing love poems "natural, [but] it was the possible outcome that alarmed them" (188).

This emergency plunge into autobiography, as revelatory as it is, results in merely a stopgap performance—something toward which Green was impelled by his pressing desire to write but something about which he did not care to deal so explicitly. His bag remains unpacked—or only hurriedly and partially packed. His greater realization as a writer was yet to come when, instead of military service, he spent the war in the Auxiliary Fire Service in London where he experienced the horrors of the Blitz. Finding himself a survivor with time to write, he produced *Caught*, a novel of far more tension and anxiety than he could express before.

CHAPTER 7

Traps: Darkness and Fire

*C*AUGHT (1943) is distinguished, if for no other reason, because of the circumstances of its composition and publication; for, in it, more than in any other novel, Green demonstrates his singular ability to write amid periods of extreme distraction and still keep his objectivity and consistency under control. The passage of time is said to be necessary for a writer to achieve proper perspective on his subject, but Green gained an esthetic distance on World War II, in particular the Blitz, while in the middle of it.

According to *Pack My Bag* Green had suffered extraordinarily few traumas while growing up. Indeed, for one so strongly motivated to write novels, his life was surprisingly quiet, though there is no doubt that his observational powers were always operative. The war, then, was his greatest known trauma; and he showed its mental, physical, and spiritual effects almost immediately. Not only did he feel these influences, but he also used them in his fiction. John Lehmann, who was publishing Green at this time, writes that a fortunate accident for literature placed Green in the Auxiliary Fire Service during the war. Though he must have been frequently exhausted and liable to be called upon at all hours to fight fires during the bombings, Green nevertheless began the opening chapters of *Caught* and produced the short sketches called "A Rescue" and "Mr. Jonas," which Lehmann soon published.[1]

Neither "A Rescue" nor "Mr. Jonas" can safely be called a short story because both lack characterization and conclusion. Instead, they are incidents or episodes which, according to Lehmann, Green admitted were true. As in most actual experiences, the end of the situation and of the central characters is unknown. In "A Rescue," the fire brigade was delayed en route to a fire because a pedestrian had fallen into a sewer whose cover had been removed and whose opening was unmarked in the blackout. Because the man was injured, the narrator had to descend into the first level to secure him with a rope. After the fireman had raised the anonymous victim from his trap and placed him in an ambulance, they heard of him no more. Green concludes, "He may have died."[2] As a narrative of the rescue process, however, and for its sheer suspense, this vignette remains one of Green's most impressive short pieces in spite of the inconclusive ending.

In this first war writing Green establishes a major image which his work would contain throughout the war—that of the trap. In "Mr. Jonas," which also relates the freeing of a trapped person, and in "A Rescue," Green employs realistic dialogue and vivid descriptions. The process in "Mr. Jonas" is actual firefighting, and the problem is how to flood the fire without drowning Mr. Jonas, who is trapped under the debris. Finally the unspeaking Mr. Jonas is rescued, but the firefighting continues until it returns later to this rescue spot. At this point in the narratives, Green indicates that Jonas, "unassisted once he had been released, out of unreality into something temporarily worse, apparently unhurt, but now in all probability suffering from shock, had risen, to live again whoever he might be, this Mr. Jonas."[3] With this comment Green adds a dimension to his sketch which, in spite of the lack of an informed conclusion, establishes a more nearly universal point: the freed Mr. Jonas evokes the biblical Jonah and his release from the great fish.

From actual facts, Green easily moved back to fiction with *Caught* where, though the background experiences are his, the situations are narrated by an omniscient author who maintains objectivity. Green did not keep himself separate easily; in spite of his early experience with the working class, he had not before lived involuntarily in such close quarters with them. Not often in the novel but occasionally with the character Richard Roe, who derives some facets of his personality and experience from Green, does a reaction occur to the shock Green felt at this first real mergence with the working class. Nevertheless, *Caught* was Green's best critical success yet. Walter Allen made the judgment then and fourteen years later still declared that it was the best novel about the Blitz that the British had.[4] The novel strongly evokes feelings and attitudes of that time, and not the least reason for its success is Green's descriptions of firemen's drill and firefighting. The experiences and procedures of the time are faithfully rendered, but the impression made upon the author was deeper than his readers could know. Almost twenty years later he projected a book and actually published an article about firefighting during World War II.

By the time *Caught* appeared, critics were paying more attention to Green and expecting more of him. John Lehmann felt justified when, in apportioning the slender wartime paper ration for the Hogarth Press, he assigned Green's work a priority second only to Virginia Woolf's. While *Caught* contains the language, style, and proletarian interest of Green's earlier novels, it showed improvement in its directness of narration and in its accuracy of dialogue from all social classes; but Green still maintained the mysterious overtones found in his colorful descriptions with their symbolism and imagery. Unity is effected by war which, though chaotic, involves everyone in traps, tensions, and frustrations. *Caught* is, therefore, a successful novel about life under stress.

The narrative runs from the beginning of World War II in England to about the tenth week after air raids on London actually begin. The main plot that concerns Richard Roe follows him from his enlistment in the Auxiliary Fire Service when war starts through his training and the long boring wait of the "phony war" (as American newspapers called the cessation of fighting during the winter of 1939–40), into the horrors of the London Blitz, and to his trip home for recuperation from a nearby bomb blast and his nervous collapse afterward. (Green bore scars from the nervous strain caused by his own experiences during the Blitz.) Inseparable from Roe's experiences, however, are the events in Albert Pye's life until his suicide. Since Pye died before the Blitz, he does not figure in all the scenes; but he is otherwise equally important. That these two characters share the principal role in the novel is emphasized by the punning combination of their names, Pye-Roe (pyro), as an addition to the fire motif.

I *Maintenance of Themes*

Green discovered additional complexities in life and in human interactions as a result of his early war experiences. The problems affected Green so strongly that he produced a novel that is not all comic—some critics would say not at all comic—but often serious and, even more than *Party Going*, bordering on the macabre. Especially, in the case of Fire Officer Pye, gruesome details multiply along with his suspicion that he committed incest with his sister when they were adolescents. The sister, now demented, kidnaps Roe's very young son briefly and then must be institutionalized. The horror of Pye's conflicts mounts throughout the novel as he tries to cope with incomprehensible events, both professional and personal, until, not able to bear the mounting pressures, he puts his head into a gas oven and dies. In spite of the ghastly effects of the war on the London masses, Green maintains the balance necessary for keeping his attention on the individual level.

Green did not so much have to reorganize his attitude toward the classes as he had to exhibit a deepened knowledge of the human truths he had been expressing all along. The result was an intensification of his statement about individual human problems as they were created and expanded by the increased scope of human events.

A crowded Auxiliary Fire Service barracks is an excellent place to portray human loneliness. Each character harbors his own problems, many of them serious, in incommunicable solitude while caught by wartime conditions and enclosed in what Henry Reed considered to be an emotional Black Hole of Calcutta. Characters go gradually from depression to despair until Roe, as one of the few survivors, accepts himself in relation to others. Individuals become isolated from one another in spite of the crowded firemen's quarters, but they reach out to others in attempts to fulfill their needs. Pye's sister establishes this quest pattern when she abducts Roe's small son Christopher. After that, Roe seeks out Pye's driver Hilly; Pye pursues Ilse's roommate Prudence; Ilse (the Norwegian refugee) attracts Auxiliary Fireman Shiner Wright; and Mrs. Howells, the fire station's cook, tries to re-establish the family of her daughter Brid, who is fast slipping into psychosis.

The lonely individual's quest for love and happiness ranges from sex, sought with even greater abandon as the war's death threat moves closer, to the simple acceptance by one's peers that is sought by Piper, the old villain unaware of his villainy, who tries to ingratiate himself with Pye and who throws Pye off an already delicate balance by echoing Pye's instruction speeches, by gossiping, and by exposing the fatal coincidence that had placed Pye over a brigade that includes the man his sister had "wronged." The solitaries of this novel also are forced to seek the unity found in teamwork and in association against common enemies such as Germans and supervisors.

The classes forced into this temporary merger still reflect Green's concern with social dissolution. Indeed, the realization of his prophetic view was accelerated by the war rather than delayed by it. Auxiliary Fire Service men looked alike on duty, leveling the social classes. In the barracks, however, especially through Piper's gossiping, each man's class is discovered; and Roe, who is from a higher social class, is paid odious deference. Also the lower classes adapt more easily to new life and skills, but Roe suffers because he is clumsy at manual labor. More disastrously caught in the wartime accelera-

tion of class dissolution is Pye, the ordinary fireman who becomes
without appropriate preparation the officer for the duration. His
adjustment would have been easier without the worry of his sister's
mental condition and his suspicion of incest, but those who survive
must adjust or collapse. Roe adjusts, and Pye does not. The strong
individuals like Roe succeed and become stronger; Shiner Wright,
the former seaman, becomes a hero when the Blitz finally begins.
That Roe survives rather than Shiner is merely a fortune of war, for
death in *Caught* becomes real rather than figurative, as in *Party
Going*.

II   *No More Telegrams*

Though Green's descriptions are still rich and evocative, he has
dropped his telegraphic style and has improved if not increased his
dialogue, for he concentrates more on the story in *Caught* than in
Party Going and less on sheer effect. Every scene carries implications
of further meaning, but proportionately fewer scenes might be
considered symbolic rather than merely realistic portrayals of events.
Such realism does not imply, however, that the novel is concerned
only with documentary aspects of Green's wartime experiences.
Instead, he transmutes his material so that it becomes fiction invented out of the evidence from his experiences. The novel rises,
therefore, above the merely topical to the universal.

The style of *Caught*, then, is that of *Party Going* but less consciously symbolic and mysterious, and it is the style of his maturity
which he would maintain through *Loving* and *Back*. In *Caught*,
Green again provides his usual richness and color: the gardens full of
roses and blackbirds; the violets, sapphires, and whites of a dimly
lighted nightclub; and the orange, rose, and pink of London dock fires
during the Blitz. Also colorful are his images which he continues to
use much in the poetic mode. A particularly telling simile occurs
when Roe gives his sister-in-law some idea of how small the firemen
felt before the immensity of their first dock fire. "Our taxi," he says
"was like a pink beetle drawing a pepper corn" (179). One of his
metaphors also illustrates how Green can use an image for the sake of
description and yet imply more. Roe's first leave which allowed him
to return home found his familiar garden drab, dead, and depressing
in the midst of winter. The garden was "all hard mud and dead soiled
swans of snow" (26). Accustomed to finding deeper meaning in
Green's birds, we puzzle over the swans, but the evocation of

depression seems to be sufficient: Roe's depression is caused by the boredom of his Auxiliary Fire Service duty, by the insecure rapport between him and his son, and by his sad memory of his dead wife.

In *Caught*, few prolonged symbols and motifs are provided, but fire and flowers predominate. Fire reflects man's universal attitudes in its suggestion of body warmth, lust, or destruction—sometimes, as with Pye, all three at once; and sometimes, as with Roe, the body warmth and its relationship to birth or renewal overcome the suggestion of destruction. Fires are described graphically and colorfully in peacetime or in war, in the overheated firemen's quarters, or in the fireplace at Roe's house where petals of flame shower light over Roe's and Hilly's naked bodies.

The major flower of this novel prepares the reader for the overwhelming flood of images, symbols, and motifs in *Back*. In both works, the rose becomes the symbol of security as well as passion. There are roses in Roe's garden—a restrained pun in comparison to what Green does with roses in *Back*. The roses of the scene with Roe and Hilly after they have made love contrast with the snows of winter gardens as well as the prelude to love when Roe's hands "went like two owls in daylight over . . . the fat white winter of her body" (117). Roe breaks out of his isolation through his love affair with Hilly. However, roses have their thorns too, and in that they become related to fire as Roe discovers during the Blitz. "The air," he remembers, "caught at his wind passage as though briars and their red roses were being dragged up from his lungs" (179). Thus Green interweaves his two symbols and in almost a metaphysical manner relates them.

Birds appear in *Caught*, though not with the frequency found in other novels. Roe and his son find the old rook trap in their garden at the beginning of the novel. Thereafter birds occur incidentally, often linked with desire: twisted like Pye's sister, the senseless nightingale; poignant like the swallows linked with Roe's dead wife; or figurative like the owls—Roe's hands over Hilly's body. These incidental references continue sporadically until the end, when Roe remembers the pigeons at the dock fires during the Blitz, flying about burning. "Some," he recalled, "were on the ground, walking in circles into the flames, fascinated" (194). The rooks trapped or caught frame the novel about men and women caught in the circumstances of war and of their own needs. The fire is that of lust as well as of destruction; and the characters, who must encounter both, are as fascinated as the burning pigeons.

III   *Communication and Character*

Integrated with the description is an even more authentic dialogue, for everyday conversation becomes a greater preoccupation with Green, who regards communication as one of man's basic problems. Roe, from the middle class, has trouble making himself understood by his fellow Auxiliaries from the lower class. At the end, he becomes irritable when his sister-in-law cannot understand his feelings about the Blitz. Pye, originally lower class but promoted beyond his capabilities because of the emergency, cannot communicate with anyone. The cooks cannot understand his interest in their equipment when he asks whether they need anything because he simply thinks they might lack a steamer when his potatoes are not thoroughly cooked. The psychiatrist at his sister's hospital talks beyond Pye's understanding so that, instead of helping his sister, he becomes suspicious and fearful and is a hindrance. The problems of human communication are reminiscent of Chekhovian depression or of Kafkaesque nightmare.

Characters are more sharply defined by dialogue. Pye, especially, betrays his awkward combination of slyness and insecurity as he boasts of peacetime fire adventures to impress and seduce Prudence. Roe says the conventional things typical of his class, but he swears at times to impress his mates. Green reflects the impact his class felt upon being thrown unceremoniously into close contact with the proletariat, for Roe has inner conflicts which he can seldom verbalize.

Working-class dialogue, fresh even in familiar expressions, is most effective. Fire Officer Trant foreshadows more than he knows the disintegration of Pye by likening him to "a chicken that had its head cut off" (86). Mrs. Howells springs into life with Cockney exclamations like "gawd love a duck, 'urry or it'll be all gone" as she runs for a cup of "you and me" (tea) (113). Even more vivid is gossipy old Piper, with his invocations of "Mother" and his irrelevant rejoinder of "so there you are then." Shiner Wright, the old sailor, comes clear though his words are unfamiliar except for his favorite catchword "Conga." Few could miss his meaning or his character when he says something like "Conger eel chasing, cock?" (65). With his ear for everyday speech, Green virtually has his style created for him.

IV   *An Ordered View of Sanity and Psychosis*

In *Caught,* Green's narrative techniques, though as complex as ever, are more consolidated, probably by Green's experience as an

Auxiliary Fire Service man. The plot is straightforward in its clarity at the same time that it contains, in the flickering manner of cinematography, frequent scene shifts and flashbacks. Green centers the plot on a major incident related in flashbacks, the abduction of Roe's son Christopher by Pye's sister, and the human complications which the incident both causes and reflects. Christopher's abduction must be considered from several points of view, especially Roe's and Pye's after the coincidental appearance in the same fire brigade of Pye, the subofficer, and Roe, the auxiliary fireman. Their lives are so divergent that otherwise they would probably never meet again; but, since they do, the exterior and interior conflicts are set. Also to be involved to a lesser degree are Pye's mad sister; Roe's sister-in-law, Dy, who has a properly emotional reaction to the whole Pye family; and Piper, the slyly innocent old gossip who creates more havoc with Pye's emotions.

Cinematic flashbacks are not jerky, however, as in *Living*, but smoothly emphasize the continual intrusion of the abnormal on outwardly normal lives. Green is ultimately concerned with interior conflict. Roe is a widower—repressed, deprived, and frustrated—who must find balm for his loneliness (in Hilly) when he adjusts to his unaccustomed life with the working class. Pye too is lonely because his home is broken up; he is promoted beyond his ability; he is not intelligent enough to grasp what happens to his sister and to himself; his affair with Prudence provides only external balm for his loneliness; and, when he reaches out to help someone, it is the snotty-nosed brat he brings home from the street. Though well intentioned, he breaks many ordinances and has his motives misconstrued. The Pye situation becomes circular with another supposed abduction of a child, this time by Pye rather than his insane sister. By this time, the reader must question whether Pye has not joined his sister in psychosis.

Indeed, psychosis is more widespread in the novel than is at first apparent. Mrs. Howells has a problem on her hands when her daughter Brid comes home with a baby, having left an irresponsible husband who has left for the army. Brid locks Mrs. Howells's valuables in a trunk and maunders about muttering that everything went wrong after the baby came. Whether Brid is suffering from postpartum psychosis or from the shock of war mobilization which took away an already wayward husband, she still demonstrates that the abnormal in Green's novels impinges upon the normal on any social level.

Setting is more symbolically significant than in Green's previous novels both for those caught in the traps of war and lust and for the appearance and atmosphere of wartime London before and, briefly, during the Blitz. Darkness and light, dark violet and bright rose, gardens under snow and gardens with flowers alternate to show the contrast between loneliness and love, frustration and fulfillment. The abnormal life becomes the normal as the characters adapt to living under wartime conditions. They know that these conditions, if they survive, cannot last beyond the war, though they soon lose sight of the fact as they become more involved in the war and begin living for the moment. One of the most significant aspects of *Caught* is that it portrays wartime London, solidly London, but London seen most often at night in blackout. In this darkness, the city characters are trapped but hunt for each other. Release comes only in the bright fires of the bombing. Roe's excursions to the country back to his old normal prewar life are set in daylight and in the garden. Usually the snowy garden underscores the frigidity of Roe's emotional life in terms of sex and of alienation from his small son, whom he must meet over again upon each infrequent visit as a virtual stranger.

Characterizations in *Caught* are effected by all the other elements of novelistic art. Setting, plot, and style contribute in such a way that little can be spared in gaining knowledge of the characters. Green has Roe narrate a good deal in addition to the omniscient narration. Indeed by the end it has become difficult to tell the narrators apart. Though not necessarily a flaw, this confusion does contribute to the anomaly which develops in that Roe begins as the major character but later gives way to a concentration on Pye and his problems. By the end, however, Roe is again dominant. Whether this situation was the result of Green's indecision or intention, the fact remains that Green made a wise choice. In spite of Roe's own success at discovering his identity and adjusting to his new role in a lower social level, he never lives so vividly as Pye. Even some of the minor characters such as Shiner Wright, Piper, and Mrs. Howells are more vigorous and more memorable than Roe.

Because of the shock of entrapment in the strange milieu of the Auxiliary Fire Service, Green could not maintain obliquity or make his fictional counterpart, Roe, come clear. Still, Roe is the novel's dominant character, and his mind deals with the major problem of finding his true identity and ultimate fulfillment. Sexually, he is able to forget his wife and have a love affair with Hilly. Paternally, he is able to regain a father-son relationship with Christopher. The conflict with Pye and its final disastrous end, however, finally takes him away from his preoccupation with self and allows him to accept life more fully. At the end, he gruffly rejects his sister-in-law's anger at Pye because he recognizes Pye as a fellow being with insurmountable problems rather than as merely a superior officer whom he must simultaneously curry favor with and harass. Roe matures beyond a neurotic self-involvement through his experiences, but Pye becomes the major factor in Roe's awakening and so must play almost an equal part in the novel.

In Green's depth studies of the conflicts involved in the Pye-Roe relationship and in the relationship between Pye and his sister, he demonstrates his ability to deal with psychological characterization several years before his portrayal of the emotionally damaged Charley in *Back*. Pye, promoted beyond his ability in the Fire Service and continuing to act toward his superiors as he did when a regular fireman, feels compelled to ingratiate himself with his men. Their reaction is the same as his so that he is trapped in a well of non-communication, and such isolation is more than he can stand. Compounding his problems at work are his problems with his demented sister, especially after he begins to suspect that in his boyhood it was she that he had seduced one dark night rather than a neighbor girl. He can never be certain; but, what is worse, he can never articulate his secret and thus secure outside help. He wonders if his sister's reaction to her seduction causes her to abduct children and to call them hers, or if this problem is simply her ultimate reaction to spinsterhood. His questions are never answered, but their very presence is sufficient to drive her brother to suicide. In an impressively hallucinatory and nightmarish scene, Pye wanders the darkened streets of London to find whether one can recognize another person on a moonless night even at such close range as the love embrace. On one such prowl Pye, to his horror, mistakes the street brat in a doorway for a prostitute; and this incident as much as anything sets the beginning of Pye's end.

In the Fire Service, Pye's nemesis is Trant, his superior officer, who, between projects to improve his comfort at Service expense, turns out the brigades to keep them alert. His discovery that Pye is away from the station too often turns him to petty tyrannies which Pye cannot stand in his precarious emotional state. Trant's tyranny is offset by the fact that in such a stressful period everyone is apt to be unreasonable.

Piper is more vivid, for a minor character, because he is a tough old

man   this is his fifth campaign—accustomed to make his way by
slyness and hard work; but he is something of an unconscious villain.
His gossip even more than his fragrant feet makes life awkward for
Roe and for Pye. Both Piper's discovery of the weird coincidence that
links Pye and Roe and his inaccurate echoes of Pye's classroom
statements boost Pye well on his way to collapse. Piper becomes
another of Green's elderly characters whose villainy causes trouble
for the younger generation. However, Green does not judge
Piper—he does not judge any of his other characters—and the reader
feels a sneaking admiration as well as sympathy for the shambling old
figure.

Without discounting the achievements in *Living* and *Party Going*,
we could say that *Caught* was Green's best novel to this point in his
career. It has a clarity and an immediacy that are not diminished for
us by the passage of time since the London Blitz. Green gains in
psychological insight as well as in experience with common speech so
that his characterizations are more fully realized than before. Events
at times continue to take on a dreamlike atmosphere with symbolic
and other poetic implications but with more straightforward results:
the plot of this novel can exist on its own terms. With the improvement of Green's art came what remains as one of the best novels about
the early months of World War II in London.

V   *Another Lull*

If the 1939–40 phony war was boring (some Britons called it the
"Bore War"), the second lull after the London Blitz was maddening;
and Green took this opportunity to characterize the bored firemen
mostly through dialogue. "The Lull" is not clearly a short story but is
more dramatized than a sketch; for it contains seven scenes that are
mixtures of conversation, narrative, and descriptions.[5] The piece, a
tour de force, succeeds by unity of tone and theme in spite of its
scenic disjointedness. The setting is usually the firehouse bar, where
loungers make desultory conversation about dull anecdotes or continually retell their adventures during the Blitz. Any stranger causes
a flurry of talk, usually pointless. When the scene is Hyde Park on a
hot Sunday, an off-duty fireman named Henry lounges with a young
lady; she quotes French poetry to him, mostly Verlaine; and then
they go to the movies, only the narrator calls it going to the "U.S.A."
In the last scene, which is between two firemen who go to duty from
the factory where they work, they discuss the boredom of "the lull"
and the man who has had a mental breakdown from the idleness.

They also comment that Londoners, so impressed with and grateful to the Auxiliary Fire Service two years before, now seem to despise them.

Green shows that life is the same during eventful and boring periods; but the busy times, no matter how tense or frightening, bring out the best in men. During the lull, the firemen go to pieces; and the public forgets its past debt to them. Both groups have again lost their ability to communicate, and they resume their isolation. Green points out the realistic situation but, as in *Caught*, judges no one.

When Green shifted his attention from London's Auxiliary Fire Service and alternating lulls and bombings to another location to continue his study of war's influence on people's lives and on the working out of his major themes, the transfer of setting to an Irish fairy-tale castle in *Loving* must have been a relief to him.

CHAPTER 8

Love and War

THE central work of his three World War II novels and the best
Green has written is *Loving* (1945). This tighter, subtler, and
more complex example of his oblique approach to narrative is a
skillful projection of the effects of war on people who are distantly
removed from the war but who are nevertheless influenced by it.
Green, living in wartime England, imagines how the war feels to
those in neutral Ireland. Despite the stress of wartorn London, the
drabness of wartime austerity, and relief found in this imaginative
distancing of events, Green is able, as in *Caught* and the short works,
to create literature in which the characters suffer emotional and
physical tensions induced by a war background.

Loving is a love story set in the gilt and plush elegance of an Irish
castle straight out of a fairy tale but with the realistic horrors of war
always in the background. Raunce, the butler, and Edith, a housemaid, fall in love among intrigues of the servants' hall while Mrs.
Tennant, the owner, and her daughter-in-law play less impressive
roles. The heir, Jack Tennant, is at war while his bored wife beds with
a neighboring Irishman. Characters debate whether to return to
England and enter military service or visit loved ones; but, mean-
while, they succumb to irrational fears of Nazi invasion or of massacre
by the Irish Republican Army.

To set this wartime novel in Ireland may strike us as whimsical, but
Green reveals the likeliest source for such an unlikely setting in an
unpublished manuscript about the London Blitz. John Russell,
granted a look at this work during a long visit with Green, says that
this version of the war began in Ireland because Green and his wife
were there on a short vacation just before Munich. War clouds were
on the horizon, but the Irish coastal scenery, Green recalls, was
memorably beautiful. Though he escaped to the countryside in the
afternoons, he was always drawn back to the radio in the evenings.
One of these evenings, in a Cork hotel, Green describes in his vividly

anecdotal manner. A half-dozen drunken Irishmen are seated around the radio set under the delusion that they are listening to a fight in London featuring one of their countrymen. The cheering they hear, however, is from a German audience chanting hysterical *Sieg Heils* at the end of a Hitler speech. Green cannot make the Irish listeners believe they are on the wrong wavelength.[1] Ireland with its peaceful scenery becomes related in Green's mind with World War II; but, at the same time, he contrasts it effectively with wartime England and Europe because of its national neutrality.

In such a setting, an objectified rendering of wartime experience, Green bettered his efforts in *Caught* because *Loving* presents most clearly his ability to portray the lives and feelings of characters who are often far removed from himself. Here more than anywhere else Green brings his meanings into focus while still maintaining the ambiguity and mystery necessary for symbolism. *Loving* is essentially a comic novel, but it contains serious overtones about pride, vanity, greed, sex, communication, and other topics.

I   *Objectified Themes of* Loving

As James Hall observed in *The Tragic Comedians*, Green, by using the servants and owners of the castle to contrast the conditions of the lower and upper classes, constructed the paradox that those who should be enjoying life are not and that those who should not be are doing so. Part of this paradox involves the problem of human loneliness. Not incompatible with loving, loneliness is motivational; and Green provides ample evidence for man's drive to seek love and to participate in loving. The great variety of loneliness ranges from Eldon, the butler, who, at the beginning of the novel, dies alone while calling for the unknown Ellen, to Mrs. Tennant, the widowed owner of the castle, who must struggle alone to manage the large estate. Jack Tennant, her son, is away at war and will not help when he is home; and his lonely wife turns to a neighboring Irish gentleman, Captain Davenport, for solace, sexual and otherwise.

When Edith, a housemaid, catches this guilty pair in bed together one morning, she finds her own loneliness for a man so stimulated that she forces her body upon Raunce's attention when she tells him of her experience. Raunce is middle-aged and not yet married; his assistant, Albert, is just entering the age of calf love. Kate, the other housemaid, is forced to find relief with the only other eligible male about the place, Paddy, the grimy Irish lampman. Miss Burch, the housekeeper, is the elderly spinster who has not considered her status permanent until the death of Eldon. Nanny Swift, the nurse-maid, rears other people's children until age forces her to be pensioned by her employers without a backward glance of gratitude or love. The list could be continued, but these instances indicate sufficiently Green's continued concern with a theme related to that of loneliness, the quest for love.

Loving concerns, however, the action as well as the condition of loving rather than the contemplation of love in the abstract. Green creates the world of loving in miniature, for the types of loving range from the calf love of Albert for Edith to the doting love of Nanny for her charges and from adulterous heterosexual love of the captain and Mrs. Jack to hints of homosexual love between the frustrated house-maids. Everyone in his isolation and loneliness must seek love, though not always successfully or properly. Since the expression of love through loving cannot always succeed as it does between Raunce and Edith, who are unlikely vehicles for conveying the ideal, the traditional marital love of Mrs. Jack and her husband is perverted to the affair between Mrs. Jack and the captain.

The core of the book is Edith's discovery of Captain Davenport and Mrs. Jack in bed; for, from that point on, the love affair between Raunce and Edith begins to develop seriously; and references to Edith's discovery are reiterated throughout two-thirds of the book like a leitmotif. Mrs. Tennant's lost ring which Edith wants to use as an engagement ring, the doves which are traditionally birds of Venus, and Edith's I-love-you scarf with which Bert is blinded in his quest for Edith also stress loving. Paddy, of course, loves his peacocks, birds of Juno, whose cries traditionally warn of disaster.

To separate loving from the fairy-tale trappings in the novel is almost impossible as the case of pale-and-wan-fond-lover Bert illustrates. Like the Courtly Lover of many a castle tale, Bert reveals the traditional symptoms of shaking, simpering, and fainting from the beginning of the book to the point near the end when he leaves for England to join the Royal Air Force and is then like a fledgling knight upon a quest in the name of his fair lady. Moreover, Raunce grows paler and sicker as his courtship of Edith progresses, almost as if she were *la belle dame sans merci;* but theirs is basically a commonplace and proper courtship. Though the novel circles from Eldon's moan of "Ellen" at the beginning to Raunce's moan of "Edie" at the end, the novel states that Raunce did not die but eloped with Edith and lived happily ever after—and, traditionally, he is the one expected to do so.

Every character in the novel expresses loving in some way from

Miss Burch over her housemaids to Mrs. Welch, the cook, over her evacuee nephew, that other Albert often referred to as a "little 'Itler." One of Mrs. Jack's daughters says she loves little Albert, and he provides an earthy commentary on the copulating doves in the dovecote. In spite of complications, everyone must reach out of his loneliness for love and must be loving something or someone, but most do not go about loving well. Although the love affair of the butler and housemaid becomes the major and the most proper affair in the novel, the young lady of the castle is in an illicit affair. In this fairy-tale setting the roles are reversed; the moral order is turned upside down; and the social order is thus shown in a state of dissolution. Green approaches the social dissolution theme from both points of view: the working class in *Living*, the leisured class in *Party Going*, and the two extremes together in *Caught*. The reversal of roles in *Loving*, which might otherwise have been a conventional fairy tale, illustrates a fact not usually admitted—that the morality of the lower classes has always been more conventional and conservative than that of the upper class.

The servants are also taking power from their erstwhile masters. This assumption is not indicated by the small change which Raunce squeezes from the household accounts as Eldon did before him; Raunce does not even detect Eldon's system of petty blackmail employed against Captain Davenport. Nor does it include Mrs. Welch's system of padding the food bills to insure herself an adequate supply of gin. Power in this case is a matter of actual control: the servants run the castle but can leave to better themselves whenever they please; the masters are dependent upon the servants; and their own impermanence is represented by their family name, Tennant. As Nanny Swift says about the upper class, "There's big changes under way" (129). The big changes, Green shows us, have been under way for more than a decade; and the good old days of the fairy tale will not return after the war.

II *Style and Symbolism*

Green's style is especially appropriate to the Irish setting in this novel. The opulent castle is described extravagantly but no more so than is fitting for a fairy tale. Not only is there more color and detail, but there is also more symbolism and imagery. In previous novels, Green provides paragraphs of description between long scenes almost exclusively of dialogue. Indeed, the amount of dialogue was increasing and the amount of description shrinking until *Loving* was written. Here, however, Green pictures an extraordinary setting which includes "the most celebrated eighteenth-century folly in Eire that had still to be burned down," a cow-byre with milking equipment in gilded wood and columns of black marble (220). Everything which can be gilded, it seems, is from Mrs. Jack's boat-bed with its large golden oar to the leaping salmon trout in gilt which formed the door levers before that ballroom with its five crystal chandeliers and red velvet walls. That *gilt* may be spelled *guilt* is emphasized by the note about salmon trout in Eldon's notebook under the entry on Captain Davenport which can refer to a sport practiced not in the captain's stream but with Mrs. Jack in the closed-off ballroom.

Frequently, Green's imaginative description of castle, dovecote, flowers, birds, and animals hides realistic meaning; but these objects provide implications which are obviously symbolic. It is, as Giorgio Melchiori says, a form of Expressionism, "a mild abstraction reached through the emphatic deformation of realistic data."[2] Green uses birds in *Loving* to assist the development of his major symbol structures, which in turn support the thematic dissolution of the old social structures. These settled structures also include love, the search for which has now become twisted and frantic, at least in the disintegrating upper class, and somewhat elevated in the lower class, only just now coming into its own. With this theme, the peacock which that "little 'Itler" Albert killed takes on a clearer meaning. Even in death, the peacock goes around in circles, dragged about until it is stinking and decaying like the social order. Mrs. Welch buries it; Badger, the dog, digs it up and presents it to Raunce, who sneaks it out to Mrs. Welch's storeroom. When Mrs. Welch finds it again, near the end of the book, she tosses it into the boiler in the charge of Raunce's assistant, also named Albert.

The circling seems connected with what Edward Stokes thinks is the probable key symbol of the novel, Mrs. Tennant's lost ring, a circle in itself, which makes a circuitous progress from Edith to the children and back to Edith before she returns it to Mrs. Tennant.[3] By this time, the ring has touched most of the servants directly or indirectly. The final circle is Eldon's moan, "Ellen," at the beginning of the book which turns into Raunce's moan, "Edie," at the end. William York Tindall says that "circles, as we know, suggest unity and loving while obscurity of loss and return imply impermanence,"[4] and from there it is a short step to Green's theme of the basic difference between the impermanence of loving and the permanence of love.

The doves and their dovecote also are symbolic as Green uses them to give his readers an acute juxtaposition of reality and unreality (55–61). Doves are birds of Venus, therefore of love, but not in the spiritual sense exclusively. Nanny Swift, with her inane little story of "the two white doves who didn't agree," and her two naive charges, Evelyn and Moira, represent the world of unreality while the whole scene of the dovecote is one of harsh reality. The precocious Cockney lad, Albert, narrates the life cycle (birth, lovemaking, death) taking place in the replica of the Leaning Tower of Pisa, which has obvious phallic significance. The two housemaids, Edith and Kate, stand by embarrassed but interested. Ernest Jones emphasizes the scene's significance as representing strife "between sexuality and the denial that it exists; [and] between the classes." "It is also," he adds, "about beauty which is inseparable from reproductive and excremental functions."[5] The doves are mentioned several other times; they are more and more explicitly related to the Raunce-Edith love affair, and they finally merge with the peacocks.

In *Loving*, the peacocks, traditionally birds of Juno, symbolize the usual pride and beauty of a fairy-tale romance. In their other possible capacity as a sex symbol, they show the gradually evolving love affair of Raunce and Edith. Since this is the only affair that is properly and conventionally concluded, it makes these two servants the hero and heroine of an inverted fairy tale complete with a sorcerer made ignoble (the brown-toothed, leprechaunlike Paddy), who tends the symbolic peacocks, and his "apprentice" (the love-struck Kate). Another item of fairy-tale trapping is the peahen's eggs which Edith stole for a love potion and cosmetic (5); but, as the realization of her love gets nearer, she denies need of them, first faintly, with her fingers crossed (94), and later completely since she "had no more use for 'em" (212). The peacocks seem to support Raunce and Edith while they make a loud outcry against Mrs. Jack and Captain Davenport (41–42). At the end, the lovers are betrothed; and the love symbols achieve their final intermingling. The doves, made part of the inversion by signifying life's stark reality as well as idyllic love, merge with the peacocks around Edith, the realistic loved one, at the end.

Birds are not the only creatures to be mentioned in this novel which teems with life and death. The hound Badger in his embarrassment and anguish serves as the conscience of the rich. And, after the mouse is found with its leg caught in the mechanism of the weathervane, mice and rats are referred to more than half a dozen times. They are unlikely if not mysterious in the ornate castle setting except for at least two possibilities. First, the weathervane and its mouse emphasize the guilt of Mrs. Jack as the arrow points to the nude figures; the discovery of the mouse causes Edith to faint in Raunce's arms—a crucial event in their courtship. Here, as in earlier instances, the mouse is associated with phallic symbolism, especially in a repugnant or evil sense; and several subsequent references are to two-legged mice and involve guilt such as for the theft of Mrs. Welch's waterglass. Second, the trapped mouse, as it suggests a character under enchantment in many a fairy tale, is after all appropriate to the novel's setting. The mouse responds to Edith's shriek with a paper-thin scream of its own as if it were more than just a mouse. In both readings mice and related matters may recur for emphasis. Green's style, often ornate, is too intentional for a reader to dismiss something this frequent as merely an insinuation.

In Green's colorful description of the "shadowless castle of treasures," he provides flowers that play a smaller part than animals; but they, as well as animals, reinforce the inclusion of death in the novel since they are static or lack the activity of animals. Especially is death emphasized when Raunce stops to dip his fingers in a bowl of potpourri, "the dry bones of roses" (64). Indeed, life and death become related to loving with the closing of eyes. Characters are seen in sleep, a couterfeit of death, and similarly in blindness, using the cliché, "love is blind" especially in a game of blindman's bluff in which the blindfold is the previously mentioned scarf printed all over with the words "I love you." Mrs. Jack has given the scarf to Edith, who is pursued in the game by Bert until Raunce interrupts. Even ruling out the meaning of the word "death" in the conventions of Courtly Love, Green has shown that the human importance of loving ranges from life even into death. But ironically, death and decay, here, also refer to the old social order and to those like the Tennants caught in its collapse.

The dialogue in *Loving* again reflects Green's uncanny ear for colloquial talk, especially that among the servants. The Chekhovian quality of incommunicability increases not just between classes but, in times of stress, among members of the same class. Dialogue also reveals individualized character; for the Tennants' literate, upperclass speech is not the same as that heard in the servants' hall where the grammar is poorer, the colloquialisms richer, and the dropped h's more frequent. However, Mrs. Tennant and her daughter-in-law are the only members of the upper class who converse much in the novel. They waltz about with meanings because, though cordial enough, they illustrate the old idea that two women of different generations cannot coexist in the same household. In fact, their tensions gradually increase as Mrs. Jack becomes guiltier about her affair with Captain Davenport.

However, Green creates an interesting ambiguity here. Mrs. Tennant compliments Mrs. Jack's strength during the absence of Mr. Jack, and Mrs. Jack reacts nervously. The reader, knowing the younger woman's unfaithfulness, is aware of the irony. What Green leaves unspecified, however, are Mrs. Tennant's ambiguous responses such as, "There is something behind all this, Violet. It's detestable." Is she speaking solely of the servants' erratic behavior or also of Violet's adultery? Violet doesn't know, and neither does the reader, but both are left to ponder Mrs. Tennant's announcement: "I shall get to the bottom of it." And she says with a grim smile at Violet's back, "I shall bide my time though"(224).

A bar to Mrs. Tennant's communication with her servants is her custom of calling the first footman Arthur no matter what his name is; for she is denying not just the servants' individuality but their very humanity. Raunce has his misunderstood conversations with the vague Mrs. Tennant; but, when Mrs. Tennant awakens to purpose and descends to converse with the cook, she finds complete non-communication because Mrs. Welch both fears wildly for her pots and pans and secretly consumes gin. A moment of high comedy, the conversation, begun with cordiality, ends with Mrs. Tennant's parting ultimatum, "If I ever find you like it [drunk] another time you'll go on the next boat d' you hear me, even if I have to cook for the whole lot of you myself" (195). Further confusion is caused by Edith's refusal to take credit for finding the lost ring even after Raunce has prepared Mrs. Tennant to thank her for it. No wonder Violet finds her mother-in-law crying some days later; it is not just because Mr. Jack has embarked for the front.

The servants have the upper hand in these conversations, but moments of tension also emphasize their individual isolation. For example, when an insurance investigator calls about the ring and can get nowhere, Bert, to protect Edith, chivalrously admits taking it. A beautiful conversational counterpoint results when Miss Burch, the housekeeper, takes tea with the cook, who is taking gin. There is also a serious note when Miss Burch, avid for gossip, tries to tell Nanny Swift that her dear Violet, whom she had reared as she is now rearing Voilet's daughters, has been found in bed with Captain Davenport.

Nanny's frenzied attempts to ignore Miss Burch's hints are ironic when compared with the inane love story she told the children at the dovecote.

Accentuating the isolation felt by all the English characters as strangers in a strange land is their utter inability to understand Paddy O'Conor, the Irish lampman. Only Kate can understand him through loving, and she must interpret even to the other servants. Mrs. Tennant describes the distance between the classes and mistakenly lumps all servants together when she tells Violet, "But my dear it's not for us to understand O'Conor." Later she states, "Of course Raunce was lying. He understands perfectly what O'Conor says" (224). Inevitably isolation increases even as individuals reach out to others for support. Only loving can facilitate communication.

Loving is the most carefully plotted and most coherently structured of Green's narratives, partly through fairy-tale conventions which, because of their inversion, support realistic rather than fantastic character portrayal. Fairy-tale elements also help form the circular structure of the novel. It begins "Once upon a day" and ends with "lived happily ever after," and within this conventional frame are the circling objects such as rings and dead peacocks. With the order and unity imposed by these circular elements, Green has less occasion than in earlier novels to use cinematic devices. Theodore Kalem, however, notes several uses of montage and camera angles.[6] Scenes flash into view as if ordered by a scenario, but they do not flicker like silent films as in *Living*. Instead, the scenes are longer and have transitions such as the screaming, running, or parading peacocks to draw the reader's attention from one group of characters to another that is just entering.

III   Loving *Characters*

Green does more in *Loving* than in his earlier novels to make his characters into real individuals. They are not only united by the common bond of loving but are also separated by loving; and they expose a specific existence through dialogue, action, and description; and the servants are more fully portrayed than their masters. For example, fuller characterization than that of Captain Davenport or Mr. Jack is given Raunce's Albert, who is hardly more than an adolescent, who is infatuated with Edith. Raunce treats him like a son or younger brother; he advises him about important matters ("You should clean your teeth before ever you have anything to do with a

woman" [3]); and he is deeply hurt when the lad runs away to join
the armed forces in England. Albert's role is also important in the
novel's fairy-tale background; for he, more than all the other male
lovers in the novel, is a traditional languishing lover. He is not
destined to succeed, however, because he can only win the affection
of the children's donkey. His departure to war means much less to
Edith than to Raunce, whose identification with the lad is emphasized by a similar languishment.

Raunce is the central character in this tale of loving, and a more
varied personality was never delineated by Green. After Raunce's
leering boastfulness to Albert about the French maid, Raunce becomes the bully of Edith and Kate ("The little bitches, I'll show 'em")
and finally the love-sick swain who moans as the birds flutter about his
loved one. He conscientiously writes his mother (who never replies)
and sends her money orders, though how he gets them is a mystery
since he never leaves the castle. Paradoxically, he also filches the
notebooks from the dying Eldon's room in order to learn how to
juggle the castle accounts, but he is more successful in loving than in
juggling accounts. How this comic butler with eyes of different colors
becomes the betrothed of the pretty young housemaid develops into
the principal concern of the novel.

Edith, the fairy princess to Raunce's Prince Charming, is remarkably self-possessed where the traditional fairy-tale heroine is emotional; and where the princess waits for her true love to happen along,
Edith calculatingly launches a plan to capture Raunce, first with
charms of peahen's eggs and later with charms of her own. Even
though she forces Raunce's awareness of her body after discovering
the captain in Mrs. Jack's bed, she is always aware of it herself, as in
the physical encounter with Kate and in the flirtatious teasing of
Raunce's Albert.

Of all the characters in *Loving*, Edith is the most loved and loving.
Miss Burch is loving toward her two maids; Kate and Edith lounge
half nude in their room; and Albert is moonstruck over Edith. Even
Mr. Jack Tennant once made a pass at her; Raunce, the repressed, is
slower to develop a love for her; but Edith brings it about. As a
reverse love goddess, she is without qualms, within the limits of her
morality, to attract the man she wants and even to steal the
waterglass, the eggs, and, during a moment of temptation, Mrs.
Tennant's ring, almost. Her one scene of emotion without ulterior
motives is the last one in which she blinks tears of happiness during
the ceremonial tableau with the doves and peacocks. Here the

realistic lovers, Edith and Raunce, have agreed to escape from the fantasy world of Kinalty Castle into the reality of England.

With all her calculation and deviousness, however, the practical Edith is much more attractive than the spoiled Mrs. Jack who much more blatantly violates the moral code of her society. Whereas Edith calculates and plans her life, Mrs. Jack indecisively wanders in and out of her affair. Edith is frank, at least to her peers; but Mrs. Jack is usually a hypocrite, not just to her mother-in-law and her husband but even to her lover.

The portrayals of the elderly women who are also loving, but more hopelessly so, are both comic and tragic. Nanny Swift is kept from retirement by wartime labor shortages and must care for the two daughters of Mrs. Jack; Mrs. Tennant, the remnant of an outworn society that is trying to carry on alone, loves her children and grandchildren; she finds strength greater than many of the characters; but she is defeated by an innate impracticality that causes her to lose as much as she gains. Even the drunken cook, Mrs. Welch, is loving, at first her scullery maids, then her pots and pans, her waterglass, and her gin. Finally, her voice grows "thick with love" for Albert, supposedly her nephew, but rumored to be her own child. Again, in loving as in living, Green gives these and other characters problems of communication among themselves, not only between social levels but also—and especially—between generations.

In the balance of character, structure, theme, dialogue, and scene, *Loving* stands as Green's best novel after which, as Walter Allen comments, Green's talent gradually becomes fragmented. *Loving* bridges the depth of the war and brings Green to its end, the time of buzz bombs, and to his next novel. In *Back*, he deals with the wounds of war, the problems of return and aftermath, and the white-collar middle class which he had hitherto more or less ignored.

CHAPTER 9

Returning

*B*ACK (1946) is, on the whole, a successful rendering of the situation in England during the last year of World War II; for Green quickly presents the problems of rehabilitation with his main character, a soldier who had fought, been wounded and captured, and, after several years, been exchanged and repatriated. The novel encompasses what appears to be the winter months of 1944–45; and, since the book was published in 1946, the actual composition must have taken place, at least partly, during the war or shortly after it ended in Europe on May 8, 1945. The date is an important part of the novel since Charley Summers, who has lost a leg and suffered the rigors of a German prison camp, must finish the war as a civilian among civilians. He is back but not simply as a returned man; he must also reap returns which come back to him from his past life, especially from Rose, his mistress, who had died during his imprisonment. His adjustments become at least threefold: to the continuing war, to his artificial leg, and to civilian life. By this simple arrangement of events, Green allows Charley's problems to expand from the particular to the universal.

Green is personally, though indirectly, involved with Charley Summers's predicament. Charley is not Green, just as Richard Roe in *Caught* is not Green; however, in *Back*, Green is again commenting obliquely on his own wartime experiences. Charley is faced with two large problems of particular significance to Green himself. First, the complexity of industrial management in a country under siege is in itself enough to drive a normal man to desperation. The difficulties a company faces manufacturing its products during wartime are sufficient, what with manpower shortages, bombed factories, and the like; but to these problems must be added the frustrations of dealing with government agencies which loom threateningly in the background. The people who have known such agencies throughout the war refer to them offhandedly by their initials; to Charley, who

101

has known them only in the last days of the war, they are mysteries. Green again reaches toward Kafka as he distributes fictitious initials for which there are no titles, "S.E.C.O.," "S.E.V.B.," and "C.E.G.S.," throughout the book. At times, the ministry is invoked as a final authority in the same fashion as Kafka might refer to the castle.

Second, the character Charley and the author Green have emotional breakdowns as a result of the war. Green has told John Russell about his own emotional upset as a result of his experiences in the London Blitz, and Russell, in "There It Is," draws the parallel with Charley and his wartime traumas.[1] However, Green takes an oblique and objectified view of his world and his problems by creating distance between himself and his character. Charley's war traumas are experienced in combat and overseas, and his background is definitely middle class, lower than Green's. Also, Green surely did not experience the deepening psychosis which Charley does after meeting Rose's look-alike, half-sister Nancy and after suffering the delusion that Rose is not dead but is rejecting him or is herself mad. Still, Green, for all his analytic examination of Charley's delusions and fixations, demonstrates more than the usual sympathy in his poetic expression of Charley's emotional disintegration and at least partial reintegration. Green stands aside to get back to himself.

I *Themes*

In a personal but objectified relationship to his novel, Green integrates his themes more thoroughly than before so that each thematic representation possesses the same value as the others. In this one instance, Green maintains a limited omniscient point of view; for he examines not the thoughts of all his characters but only those of Charley Summers. Others are known mostly from the exterior, though occasionally Green says that Mr. Grant, Rose's father, is flabbergasted or James Phillips, her husband, is a kindhearted man. Major attention is upon Charley and his problems, which are loneliness and isolation; the quest for identity through human relationships, especially love; and the dissolution of the old social structure.

No one is more alone than Charley when he first returns from Germany; for he is isolated by his war experiences, by the loss of his leg, by his long absence from civilian life, and by the death of Rose. In addition, he was a lonely figure even before the war; he was a bachelor with few friends and was not much thought of by them.

Used by the self-centered Rose and relegated to a minor executive post in his company, he was a nonentity whom no one would notice in a crowd.

War, however, isolates many people. James Phillips is left, after Rose's death, to rear their son in a small-town backwater. Mrs. Grant, Rose's mother, retreats into the protective isolation of amnesia to avoid facing the war and her daughter's death. After Nancy Whitmore's mother (whom we never meet) has been evacuated, Nancy, Rose's illegitimate half-sister, lives in her apartment with only her cat for company. Dot Pitter, Charley's secretary, is alone; Arthur Middlewitch, also a returned veteran, is alone; even the very married Corker Mead, Charley's boss, is portrayed alone in his office. The aim of the book, however, is to deal with Charley's problems and, ultimately, with Nancy's as they move together.

The quest for love becomes as important a thematic concern in *Back* as is human isolation; and love is, of course, the solution to the latter. The complication with lonely Charley is that love is dead because Rose is dead; but, when he finds Nancy and thinks she is Rose, his troubles really begin. In his delusion, he is more isolated than ever and cannot make even the simplest contacts with others. Mr. and Mrs. Grant use him as a foil for their own problems; Middlewitch finds him a bore; and, after Charley hesitates about sleeping with Dot Pitter, he finds that James has already bounced into bed with her.

In addition to the sexual implications of the quest for love, Green integrates religious references. Perhaps because the omnipresent Rose reminds him of the Christian significance of the flower, Green uses clear biblical allusions for the first time. Charley denies Rose three times in the course of the novel for no particular reason than that three denials is an effective number and that Charley must somehow get his dead mistress out of his system. The allusion is successful in that it raises Charley's problem from a particular erotic fixation to a universal problem of adjustment to the death not only of a person but also of the past. This adjustment Charley must accept, and he is successful to the extent that his futile search for a dead love becomes the birth of a new one. The dead past is not completely forgotten—Charley calls Nancy "Rose" even as they lie on their bed of love at the end of the novel—but he at least learns to accept his past in a way that allows him a new beginning in which he will both find himself and end his isolation.

The problems of other characters are not so clearly solved. Mrs.

Grant regains her memory, though with the loss of her husband; James Phillips remains a widower, and his son remains motherless; Dot Pitter finds another secretarial job. Although these characters seem to have accomplished little progress, they keep striving as if they have not reached the point of futility. This indomitability is typical in Green's characters: they continue functioning, often in lively fashion, and ignore the futility looming before them.

In *Back*, Green provides only middle-class characters, so that social dissolution is portrayed here not in terms of social classes but in terms of wartime stresses and confusions. Besides the clear cases of mental imbalance in Charley and Mrs. Grant, milder problems are faced by almost every other character from Middlewitch to Mead. As James Phillips tells Charley after their disastrous confrontation of Nancy, "this is the war." And he explains, "Why only the other day in my paper I read where a doctor man gave as his opinion that we were none of us normal" (89). In the wartime confusion, frustration, human loss, and dislocation, the people's material possessions, orderliness, and security of a rooted existence all are destroyed. Nothing will be again as it was before the war. Charley gets little help from anyone because everyone needs help.

II *A Rose Is Not*

The style of *Back* is clearly Green's though it is sparer than in the elaborate descriptions of *Loving*. Green still provides poetic intricacy, as in his two descriptions of gardens and in his involved play on the word *rose,* but he also balances better his tendencies toward poetry and authentic dialogue. Not yet to the point of reducing summary and description to the barest minimum, he has progressed beyond the jerkiest of his cinematic scene shifts; but Green's style retains the terse short sentences except when he embellishes the plot with descriptions of gardens. In each case, the garden provides metaphors for love and for Charley's quest for love. The novel begins with Charley's visit to the graveyard, the garden of death, where his love lies buried. Later in the book, he and Nancy visit the garden of the bombed house. Both man and garden have suffered wartime damage, but this time his love is alive. At the end, Nancy welcomes Charley to her bed for a premarital experience; and, as in the two gardens, the scene is described as a bower of roses.

In this novel Green uses flowers rather than birds for his major symbolism and imagery. The rose, which permeates the book, adds color, richness, and mystery. Henry Green dares what few novelists would undertake in using the word *rose* almost to the point of monotony, but he carries it off well. Not only as a flower is the word used but also as a proper noun, a color, and even a verb. The gardens are full of roses; Charley's mistress was named Rose; colors range from red to ivory pink; and, as Mrs. Frazier says, wartime prices "rose, they've rose . . ." (35). There are roses on cheeks and breasts and even on wallpaper. Everywhere Charley turns, there are real or imagined reminders of his lost love.

Reinforcing the name, Rose, with that of the flower is Green's punning use of interlocking proper names that usually involve roses but progress in color from rose to white. Rose Phillips is the dead mistress, the last rose of summer for Charley Summers. Charley Rose is a name mentioned to Summers by Arthur Middlewitch, a nonentity who is sandwiched into the middle of Summers's problems. The dead husband of Rose Phillips's half-sister Nancy is Phil White; and his widow, Nancy, resumes her maiden name of Whitmore. The interrelated significance of this word play is that Charley comes back to his fixation any way he turns, but his ultimate salvation lies in his progress from the rose-red of chaos and lust to the white of peace and purity. Other than presenting the serious theme, Green is having a quiet joke at the readers' expense, just as he does in his diversionary tactics in other novels: reusing his symbolic words in regular dialogue and using the name or similar names for several characters such as the two Alberts in *Loving* or Charley Rose and Charley Summers in *Back*.

If flowers tend to symbolize stasis as birds symbolize change, *Back* is to be interpreted as the quest for stability, initially through a return to the past. But, though the person can come back physically, he cannot turn back time. Charley must attain stasis by making a new life, ironically by gaining the love and companionship of a highly elusive woman, Nancy, who is not quite ready for a static life with Charley Summers. She, however, must initiate the relationship with the befuddled Charley.

Since the aim of this novel is stasis, Green's birds of change have only an incidental role. Mostly they are geese, appropriately enough, because one character or another is always in a honking panic or a silly stupor. Parabolam, the product of Charley's firm, is made from bird droppings. As if to guarantee a minor role to birds, Green provides a larger role to Nancy's cat, the nemesis of birds. This book is about love, marriage, and sex; and the cat, Panzer, is fecund. As Panzer swells in pregnancy, Charley and Nancy's love grows until even a word play on reds and roses cannot deflect Charley from his new intention (170).

III   *Talk and Memory*

In spite of Green's word play, his dialogue is again remarkably accurate as colloquial speech, so accurate that critics have had cause to consider it monotonous and dull; but there are legitimate reasons why such potential handicaps do not ruin the novel.[2] Green, as usual, individualizes his conversations so that the characters do not talk alike; and he also uses dialogue to express much of the confusion and self-preoccupation in Charley as well as in the other characters. Since, for example, the wartime noise, strain, and destruction draw each person into himself, Dot Pitter rattles on even when, at James's house, she cannot be heard above the rumble of lorries on the road outside. James and Charley make little effort to understand her, being themselves so preoccupied. When Mrs. Grant loses her memory as self-protection from the war, her husband discusses her case in her presence as if she were absent or at least deaf; and Mrs. Grant treats her husband the same way when he is paralyzed by a stroke.

For much of the novel, Charley is so confused or self-concerned that he can scarcely have a communicative conversation. When someone triggers his preoccupation by mentioning Rose, he turns everything off but that; even when Mrs. Frazier tells him the story of Rose and Nancy, Charley pays no attention, being mesmerized by that key word (34). Until Nancy's true identity is finally confirmed to him (155), Charley can never converse with Nancy as Nancy. Everything she says he greets with sly qualification; he is convinced that she is Rose in disguise, Rose turned prostitute, Rose gone mad. Charley's preoccupations, then, lead him into conversations that are monotonous, one sided, or uncommunicative in the Chekhovian manner. For instance, when selfish Charley meets selfish Arthur Middlewitch at lunch, neither is interested in the other, nor do they listen to each other. Charley claims to have had a child by his former mistress, but all that the womanizing Middlewitch catches is Charley's mention of the widow to whom Mr. Grant has referred him: " 'A widow.' Mr. Middlewitch echoes. 'Oh boy. I say remind me to go across to Ernie Mandrew when we're through, will you? I've got a bit of news that will interest him, only I'm so damned forgetful these days. What were we saying?' " (26). The breezy chat of Middlewitch does not penetrate the barriers of Charley's problem, and Charley retreats again into himself.

IV *Circle and Return*

The plot of *Back* is another circular pattern, but Green does not form or close the circle so thoroughly as he does in *Loving*. The development of the plot, however, is the development of Charley; at least, change occurs. Charley, who is in a state of confusion at the beginning and is having difficulty accepting reality because of horrible war experiences and the death of Rose, gradually begins to accept his state after visiting her grave until he meets Nancy, the half-sister of his dead mistress and her double ("alike as two peas" in Mrs. Frazier's words) except that Nancy's hair is black and Rose's was, of course, red. Because he thinks Nancy is Rose in disguise, his disorientation increases rapidly to the point of neurosis or beyond. When, through the illness and death of Mr. Grant, he gradually must face the truth about Nancy's identity, he gradually reenters the world of reality and self-discovery.

At the peak of his confusion, Charley is given a story about just such a case of mistaken identity; for James Phillips has learned the truth about his friend's problem and is trying, subtly, to help his old rival. In this instance, Green could be accused of a false step, for the interpolated story, from eighteenth-century France, is a bromide among expository techniques. But Charley is beyond subtle hints and even bromides, just as he is beyond listening to Mrs. Frazier's explicit description of the case of Rose and Nancy. The story is not inserted to help Charley; it does not. It is placed there to show the depths of Charley's delusion, and at this point nothing so bland can help him.

What Charley must learn comes from experience and shock, and even those are insufficient for a final cure. Thus the circles from Rose to Rose and garden to garden lead only back to themselves rather than out of the chaotic wartorn world. Charley enters the garden of death at the beginning and accepts Nancy's love in the shattered but living garden near the end; but, just as he is seeking Rose at the beginning, he calls for Rose as he takes to Nancy's bed at the end. Green provides a realistic appraisal of the price each individual must pay as a result of war, and he does not provide a final resolution of what in life is rarely resolved.

Whereas Green's earlier works flickered in brief and sometimes jerky fashion like old silent films, *Back* focuses longer on individual scenes and affords smoother transition. Without altering his method completely, Green retains a cinematic definition while providing chapter divisions, though untitled and unnumbered. At the same time, his settings, except for the gardens, are compressed into fewer descriptive passages. Some of the interiors are evoked rather than detailed: Charley's office, the restaurant, James's house, and Nancy's flat. The result is effective rather than merely sparse. In London during the buzz-bombing, life was in limbo since the destruction was more haphazard than the earlier bombings. There was no logic to it, just fate. The same is true of the village where Phillips and Mandrew live, a quiet backwater but one also susceptible to the random fall of a buzz bomb. Also, Green's emphasis is on people.

V *Confused People*

Characters in *Back* are living people; but, as we have observed, Green provides only Charley's interior life since others are revealed mainly through dialogue with occasional authorial comment about what a person thinks or feels. When the author relates what Charley observes, we must interpret this narrative according to what we know about Charley's emotional stability at the time. For example, Charley sinks toward emotional darkness as he meets each character in his progress back to civilian life, but Green's most effective means of portraying Charley's disintegration rather than the confusion of interpersonal relationships is the nightmarish, almost surreal recurrence of the word *rose*. Green, without being clinical, provides a psychological study of Charley's fears and suspicions that is almost Freudian.[3] Charley is already inadequate to life's demands, but the losses of his leg and his mistress, both sufficient to imply castration, lead him in a retreat from life often described as an attempt to return to the womb. Charley is the little man who comes through the horrors of war wounded—he knows not how badly—but who is still striving for a life. He becomes a minor Everyman, transcending his individual predicament.

Characterization of Nancy is another of Green's accomplishments mainly through dialogue but with some meaningful actions. She is defensive because of her illegitimate birth and the loss of her husband in the war. These experiences give her a brusque veneer which covers real sympathy for and understanding of a wounded person. That she ultimately accepts Charley, who is only half a man, is no surprise.

More interesting in the process is Green's handling of the Rose-Nancy mistaken identity, for Nancy is characterized to a large extent by comparison with Rose, both directly and through the persistence of Charley's delusion. During much of the novel, all things that Nancy says and does are, to Charley, the utterances and actions of Rose. To do this Green must also expose Rose's character retrospectively. While Charley's memories of her are, he believes, sweet ones, she is shown to be selfish and unfeeling. She takes as much advantage of her lover as she does her husband. Charley's few love letters from her are not love letters at all but written evidence of her lack of love. Rose did not cause Charley's withdrawal from life—it is important to see that he is not strong-minded in the first place—but she did exercise tyrannical control over him. The irony is two-edged when her cold letters are cut to pieces; for Charley, to cull a sample of her handwriting for expert comparison with Nancy's, snips off every word or phrase he considers too personal for the handwriting expert to see and blindly continues to snip until he reduces all of Rose's letters to confetti. However, Rose's words expressed contempt rather than love, and Charley has, symbolically and unconsciously, cut her to bits. All he remembers is Rose, naked in bed, laughing; but she is laughing at him.

Minor characters, like James Phillips, are provided as assistance to Charley's collapse and reintegration, but through their conversation they live as individuals. Middlewitch, who knows Charley from their days together in hospitals, tries to help; but, full of empty small talk and himself disoriented, he returns to civilian life in full pursuit of women. He vaguely feels sorry for Charley; but, without a Nancy to help him, he loses his job and ends up worse.

The elderly act as unwitting tyrants to the young. Like Mr. Craigan in *Living* and Piper in *Caught*, the Grants and those of their age burden Charley Summers or take advantage of him. Mr. Grant sends Charley to Nancy for selfish reasons, and both Mr. and Mrs. Grant use Charley as therapy when he cannot cure himself. Mrs. Frazier, who knows the secret of Grant's love affair, hoards the coal and tries to get Charley, by virtue of his wounds, to go to the head of the queues and do her marketing. Green unhesitatingly mixes humor and seriousness when Charley's boss, Corker Mead, is ready with bad advice and with lectures on the efficacy of marriage. Immediately afterward, he picks up the telephone and argues with his wife. No one consciously wishes Charley ill; like all Green's characters, they are enthusiastically involved in living as if they did not know that the deck is stacked against them.

As an artistic whole, *Back* deserved more favorable critical comment than it has received. In unity of structure, evenness of style, and exactness of characterization, the novel stands with *Loving* and *Caught* among Green's best. What critics have called "clumsiness" is more a rendition of Charley's confused mind which reflects the chaos of a disintegrating social structure. The dullness of the characters' lives and conversations is realistic, but a more important advantage is that such commonplaceness overlies the tensions of people on the brink of madness. On a literal level, *Back* is the description of a wounded soldier back from the war; and it is one of the few World War II novels which treat this return and the difficulties of readjustment to civilian life without sentimentalizing what is really hard truth. Green takes a painfully average man, confronts him with as many problems as most men confront, but does not say that the problems must be the same for everyone. After dealing with the closing days of World War II, Green, who allows Charley a substantial recovery, indicates hope for the future. Since the election of a Labour government at the war's end did not seem so hopeful to a manufacturing executive, he wrote his next novel, *Concluding*, about the implications of a life under socialism.

CHAPTER 10

Not the End

*C*ONCLUDING (1948) is neither Green's last novel nor a definitely concluded one. By projection, however, the novel, because it is set in the future, does conclude the chronicle of Green's times and perhaps his own life. Simultaneously, *Concluding* also follows Green's previous novel, *Back*, in a logical historical sequence. These descriptions of *Concluding* are neither paradoxical nor contradictory; they are the results of Green's habit of writing about events close to the time of their occurrence. In this novel, however, he carries the events to a possible culmination and sets the book in that future period. In fact, *Concluding* was influenced in its composition by the end of the war and by the onset of inevitable reactions that would affect the future. The British public had reacted by electing a Labour government headed by Clement Attlee, who replaced Winston Churchill at the Potsdam Conference after July 25, 1945. Individually, British citizens like Henry Green were thinking about the future.

Green's other novels are set in the present or the recent past, but *Concluding* is set in a future in which, as the title indicates, the society Green knows has already dissolved; and he mirrors his worst fears that individuals will become lost in the mass. Society has been leveled to the extent that servants are equal to masters or in control of them. Nevertheless, the novel's emphasis is still on life in all of its rich variety, as Edward Stokes has noted, rather than on a political anti-Utopia.[1]

Relevance to Green himself is again present in his novel, though as usual without any directly autobiographical implications. Still, two personal elements probably motivated him in the composition of *Concluding*. First, Green, as Yorke the capitalist, naturally would consider the darker implications of a Labour government. His prediction is not encouraging in its portrayal of life lived by arbitrary rules and bureaucratic inhumanity. He does not eliminate humanity,

111

however, since he gives his characters sex as an outlet; but this sex is less elevating than it might be. In the futuristic or anti-Utopian sense, *Concluding* is related to Orwell's work and before it to Aldous Huxley's, though Green differs by focusing more on the people's condition than on the political structure.

Second, Mr. Green and Mr. Rock, the elderly protagonist, had some personal similarities. Both protected their individual privacy: Green did so by trying to prevent anyone from photographing his face; Rock, by placing all of his mail, unopened, into a trunk. Since both men were deaf, each must attend to problems of communication. Both men were elderly at about the same time: Rock, by description; Green, by setting his novels in the future of his own old age. The future setting is convenient for disguising contemporary references to problems of the sexes, of the generation gap, and of the state versus the individual. Green also reveals the natural tendency of the middle-aged man to theorize upon his old age. At the same time, he maintains his oblique viewpoint by use of the futuristic setting and by the absence of a familiar class structure.

The novel is set on an old estate that includes a mansion-turned-state-school, several cottages, a mysterious forest swarming with birds, and a lake that perhaps contains a body. Characters search fruitlessly for Mary, a runaway student; Mr. Rock fears the loss of his cottage; and Elizabeth and Sebastian have an affair. All the action is fascinating but unconcluded.

I *Thematic Concerns*

One of the most interesting aspects of *Concluding* is the extension of Green's major themes into the future. Admittedly, the future reflects the past so that Green is not merely prophesying but is providing an esthetic distance from which to view the present. And, to an even greater extent than in *Back*, he utilizes action, symbolism, and imagery to expose his thematic concerns. This novel, even with its moments of comedy, dwells on the threshold of man's negation. A possible sterilized future in which the state controls each individual's life can be faced only through the hallucinatory effects provided by symbolism and suggestive imagery. It seems almost more than Green can bear to imagine that man's worst fears will be realized; that—in spite of man's striving for identity, security, and personal relationships—he will not merely remain but will become more isolated, unloved, and deprived of a comfortable place in an equitable society. The novel makes us feel that these developments are possible and that they have evolved logically from the conditions exposed in Green's previous works.

Human isolation and loneliness are intensified in *Concluding* as in other Green novels by the conflicts between youth and age and between the related desires for change and maintenance of the status quo. Mr. Rock, the oldest character, is a man who, though a famous scientist years ago, has outlived all his contemporaries and all his loved ones except a granddaughter, Elizabeth. He must fight alone for security against a system he does not completely understand. His integrity and perseverance are admirable. Still, he is fighting against change, and this role is usually assigned to the villain.

Of all living people, Mr. Rock loves only his granddaughter, and certainly not Miss Edge, who would deprive him of his home, or the cook, to whom he must act with obsequious deference when cadging a bite of breakfast. The schoolgirls merely bewilder him; they are too young and vital for his flagging energies. The remainder of his affection is reserved for his pets, the goose, the cat, and the pig; but these creatures reflect and intensify his loneliness because each is itself the lone member of its kind on the estate.

Other characters have been isolated by the rigid, dehumanizing rules which are the stultifying effects of the Welfare State. Among these individuals are those who support the state and bear up under their administrative responsibilities. They are old maids, women alone without more than the barest relationships, the Misses Edge, Baker, and sardonically, "Ma" Marchbanks. Mr. Rock's granddaughter, Elizabeth, is in her thirties and still unmarried; but she has come to her grandfather's house to recover from a nervous breakdown caused by the pressures of the system. Her lover, Sebastian Birt, is a bachelor in a school populated mostly by women and girls.

The girls at the school present a complex problem of loneliness and isolation. They are isolated from males of their own age at a time when their sexual development is beginning to demand an outlet. Trapped in an arid system, they wish to escape into the real world and find their individual identities. Indeed, one of them, Mary, does escape, at least as far as the novel is concerned. Another, Merode, is found in the woods. Returning her to the school is no assurance that she or another student will not escape later.

The girls at the institute are depersonalized by being massed together like a flock of birds. Their individual identities are nullified even by their names, usually signs of individuality, because they begin with the same letter *M* as in Mary, Merode, Moira, and

Marion. Green also begins the names of adults at the institute with the letter *B*: Miss Baker, a principal; Miss Birks, the matron; Maggie Blain, the cook; and Sebastian Birt, the economics instructor. Such an impersonal system cannot be dealt with by any other means than flight. Mary's escape at least has given her more of an identity in the eyes of her peers. The only implication of her success is the possible equation of the truant Mary with Ted, the goose, who disappears but then reappears after having gained the freedom of flight.

Green again relates human loneliness and isolation to the quest for love. Although he has used *Loving* as a title before, it could also be appropriate in this case. Indeed, in many ways the problems of love are more complex in *Concluding* than in previous novels. Love is not possible with abstractions, and this is what the state has made of its citizens. Before love can be achieved, then, a character in the novel must separate from the mass into which the state has pressed him and discover his identity. Secure and satisfying human relationships, Green indicates, come not in a large, faceless group but between two distinct individuals.

Much of the love for old Mr. Rock existed in the past. His wife is dead; however, he has not lost his need to give and receive love. His affection for his granddaughter is deep and jealous though her return for his love is selfish and erratic, partly as a result of her nervous breakdown and partly because she is otherwise obsessed with her love for Sebastian Birt. Rock is not oblivious to the beauty of youth as the girl students flaunt their charms before his failing eyes or kiss his dry lips, but he cannot reciprocate in this kind of love and scorns Miss Edge's marriage proposal. His quest for love continues only for his granddaughter, for his pets, and, in a sense, for his cottage, which provides all the peace and security he knows.

Elizabeth seeks love in a different way, for she and Sebastian embody their quest for love in the carnal act. James Hall considers their relationship Green's "devalued image of love," for their love affair is one between two people who are unsure of themselves or of each other. Hall believes that they will eventually marry, but with such uncompleted personalities it is difficult to be certain.[2] By the end of the novel, however, Elizabeth can think of nothing but marrying Sebastian, so her quest for love is at least clearly identifiable if not an immediately successful one.

Love, for the girls massed together at the institute, is an ultimate quest which cannot be launched successfully until they achieve individual identities. Security is not in numbers; for, because of their youth and because of their submergence into the system, they are denied the love in which security lies. None of their efforts to achieve love progresses above the subterranean: the stealth with which they kiss Mr. Rock; the whispered tale—true or false—that some of them slip out to old Adams at night; or the secret club held in the mansion's basement where they play recorded music of the days before state control. Their solution must be to run away from the mansion as Mary and Merode do.[3] As noted before, the novel ends without our ever discovering whether Mary has drowned in the lake, hidden in Adams's hut, or escaped with some rescuing Porphyro. Wherever Mary is, she leaves her schoolmates more eager than ever to end their depraved innocence and to find themselves.

Mary has other reasons for leaving the institute. Because of her industry and efficiency, many adults have put too much work on her shoulders. She is said to have told some of the girls that she has tired of perpetual servant duties. This confusion of roles relates to the theme of social dissolution as the best students of a school become servants. Edge and Baker feel such service is an honor, but the girls do not. This dissolution of society is also one of humanity.

Miss Edge loves the system, but she treads on the edge of another type of love when she speaks of the wonderful place in which her school is located. Her proposal of marriage to Mr. Rock is at first a shock even though she explains it to herself as a desperate attempt to gain control of his cottage and to maintain the system. Another possibility, however, is that she seeks a fulfillment so natural that even she cannot deny it.

II *A Culmination*

While attempting the prophetic novel, Green continues to deal with his usual themes; but, as we have suggested, *Concluding* is more a culmination than a continuation of Green's theories and techniques. Whereas his past novels contained identifiable story lines and plot structures, Green in *Concluding* draws together most of the poetic techniques which have fascinated his critics since the 1930s. To describe a future socialistic limbo, Green proceeds from real life into dreamlike fantasy; for he uses color, plant, and animal symbols and images to describe the feelings of individuals who are struggling to find their identities and separate themselves from the mass culture. In this regimented world, for instance, the representatives of the state who seek to order everything are portrayed by reducing most colors to black and white. The Misses Edge and Baker are dressed in black; the girls, in white. Baker advocates the establishment on the institute grounds of a black-and-white farm, where all of the animals will be either black or white or spotted black and white. Broadening these implications throughout the novel, Green uses contrasts of black birds against a white (or light) sky, and the progress through the novel is from night to day and back to night.

Green's purpose, however, is not simple. His interests still are involved with persons, and his persons are changeable. Sea imagery is employed occasionally to reinforce the idea of change rather than stasis and to blur the realistic picture into hallucination and fantasy. Natural objects on land often change to objects in the sea. Sebastian, for example, "parted a screen of leaves that hung before him bent to the tide, like seaweed in the ocean . . ." (56). The girls' eyes are compared to "jewels enclosed by flesh coloured anemones . . ." (109), and Mr. Rock notices that "veins of quartz in flagstones . . . appeared to him like sunlight that catches in sharp glass beneath an incoming tide . . ." (245).

Even flowers, which Robert L. Weaver relates to stasis and security, are not colorful or do not stay the same.[4] In *Concluding*, when used for party decorations, they are blighted by swarms of insects that recur almost like biblical plagues. While flowers are stacked in the dining hall, they frighten characters with their funereal implications. Some characters fear that the missing Mary's body is concealed underneath, but this fear is alleviated when only Mary's doll is found.

Birds fly again in this novel, singly and in large swarms, as Green uses them not only as poetic and structural devices but also as minor and major symbols. In his usual diversionary manner Green employs birds freely in conversational cliché and narrative transition. Miss Marchbanks, for example, tells Moira confidentially, "Besides we rely on you senior girls, you realize, before the bird is flown, so to speak, you know" (50). In other instances, birds are used to describe persons or emotions. Miss Marchbanks's worry for the two runaway girls is "like an ulcer high under the ribs, where it fluttered, a blood stained dove with tearing claws" (47). Earlier, Mr. Rock described Misses Baker and Edge as "those two State parrots" (39). Similarly, some of the birds in *Concluding* are used simply to describe times of the day, as when on page six it is early morning, too early for the birds. "The first black bird gave heed that night rode near" introduces a description of the evening (168). At last, night had fallen, and "each starling's agate eye lay folded safe beneath a wing" (187). (The

starlings used here are independent of those which apply symbolically to the characters because at this time everyone is still awake.)

Though these uses of birds enrich the novel's style and structure,
there are still other occasions when birds are clearly symbolic. As in
Living and in *Party Going*, *Concluding* has notable personal symbols;
but these are linked with the previously noted black-and-white
arrangement of rigid state laws and of right and wrong.[5] Misses
Baker and Edge are called "a couple of old black herons" (219), and
Edge is likened to "a black ostrich feather" on the dance floor (199). In
contrast, Mr. Rock is related to his white goose, Ted, who has never
flown at all but by the end of the book has startled the old man by
flying straight at him out of the darkness (252). The confusion in Mr.
Rock's head, represented by Ted's undependable wanderings
throughout the book, has been resolved into a semblance of order,
represented by Ted's flying and returning home. Mr. Rock, who has
won a moral victory over Miss Edge that night by refusing her
marriage proposal and has gotten his wits more or less straightened
out about his problems, continues to his cottage, where he finds that
the white goose is there before him. The implication is fairly clear that
Mr. Rock will keep his cottage.

Concluding has a thematic bird symbol of large scope. Here Green
presents a picture of what his civilization could become, a society in
which state control seeks to regiment and repress human life and
emotions. However, as Stokes points out, "the setting also includes
the [mysterious, bird-haunted] forest surrounding the school [which]
is equally clearly a symbol for the elemental, instinctive life which
humanity attempts to deny, but which will not be denied."[6] This idea
is implicit in Green's linking of the free-flying, swarming starlings to
the girl students. He says the girls' murmuring is "a susurration of
feathers" (21), and at lunch "the noise of their talking was a twitter of a
thousand starlings" (98). The swooping and swirling black mass of
birds is related further to the whirling white mass of girls at the dance.
Stokes says that "perhaps it all 'means' no more than that the girls still
have a grace, a freedom and an irresponsibility that their elders have
lost; it may suggest that they are closer to 'the source of life.'"[7] We
agree with this interpretation as far as it goes, but the birds do "mean"
more.

In the previous discussion, representatives of state control are
related to black birds and those against them are related to white
ones. Moreover, the starlings are extended to the other, older
characters in the novel, such as Miss Edge, who *watched* "a cloud of

starlings" rise over the woods in the morning (19). Also, Elizabeth, walking to the dance with her grandfather, watches the magnificent swarming and circling of the birds settling for the night (176–77). At the same time, she is thinking of Sebastian, with whom she has had sexual relations. A much wider application of the starlings, therefore, is not just to the girls, who seek freedom from regimentation, but to most of the other characters as well. This broadened application emphasizes especially the sexual aspect of escape from regimented, emotionless life under the state; and every person, including representatives of the state itself, *must* want to escape because of that "instinctive life which humanity attempts to deny, but which will not be denied."

This knowledge puts a definite sexual emphasis on the surging masses of starlings and recalls Liz's own jealousy inspired statement about the girls at the school: "I don't think they ought to have masters, Gapa, at these places . . . since they're only children, the girls I mean, and sex is unconscious at their age. It's such a temptation for a man" (160). So it is for Sebastian when he finds the runaway Merode lying in the woods in torn pajamas that expose "a knee which, brilliantly polished over bone beneath, shone in this sort of pool she had made for herself in the fallen world of birds, burned there like a piece of tusk burnished by shifting sands . . ." (56). Another hint of sexual implications is contained in the anonymous letter Miss Edge received: "Who is there furnicates [*sic*] and the goose" (164). This woman is the same Miss Edge who watches the starlings at the beginning and, in effect, tries to join them at the end when she proposes marriage to Mr. Rock, the owner of the goose.

In *Concluding*, the white goose Ted is the bird used to show shifts from one scene to another on three occasions. First, he announces the arrival of the policeman who has come by Mr. Rock's cottage on the way to investigate the disappearance of the girls (71–72). The second use of Ted follows in three pages when the goose's leaving prepares for the policeman's confused departure and shifts the reader's attention to Misses Edge and Baker. Finally, Mr. Rock goes to the lake to search for the lost girl and, when he finds that he is noticed by two other people, calls Ted as an excuse for his being there. The echo, "Ted, Ted," shifts the scene to the watchers on the other side of the lake (150). When these uses of the white goose are set aside, we can see Ted's significance in the last part of the novel more clearly as a symbol of resolution and order in Mr. Rock's confused life.

III *Dialogue and Deafness*

Concluding is the last novel in which Green provides a great wealth of imagery and symbolism; however, his dialogue is, as usual, amazingly accurate not only in conversational tone but also in monotony of subject matter. This time Green provides the additional complication of Mr. Rock's deafness, for he often gets as confused as he does, for instance, in his long talk with Adams (6–10). Again, when he converses with the police sergeant and is unable to hear correctly, he uses "an idiotic look, as he often did" (72). On these occasions he is similar to Sebastian Birt, who is always putting on one imitation or another. Characters' conversations fail to communicate, as in Chekhov's *The Cherry Orchard*; but the causes are different because the futuristic setting involves political as well as social changes. Mr. Rock is being wary of what he tells others, and in this sense he is no different from the state officials he loathes, Baker and Edge. When Baker is interviewed by the policeman, she intentionally fails to communicate the true situation for state reasons as well as personal ones. The policeman, also a servant of the state, knows what she is about but is wary for his own reasons (92–94). Elizabeth Rock, recovering from a nervous breakdown, is often panicky and loses track of conversations. Though she is in love with Birt, his affectations and imitations of others mingle with her easily distractable mind to disrupt communications between them (43).

In this new state-controlled society, the initials "O.M.S." appear over official communications meaning, as Green parenthetically explains, "On Majesty's Service; they had left out the His, long since, as being unworthy of the times" (33). The official letters to Rock and Edge (especially the directive she receives concerning pig farms) are full of official language, but none of it is any worse than today's "federalese." Baker and Edge do soberly discuss sitting on commissions in London, speaking to a member of the Secretariat of New Buildings, and being trustees of the girls and of the Great Place in which the institute is housed. Even Edge's surprising marriage proposal to Mr. Rock is so circuitously phrased that it takes both the reader and the honoree a while to catch her drift. Edge, however, is a mixture of sentiments about the estate and governmental directives just as Baker, who talks of black and white, weeps over her orphans (77–79).

IV   *Image and Impression*

If the novel contains much realistic talk, it also contains abundant descriptive images, some of action but mostly ones of setting. Green employs imagistic poetic techniques so that *Concluding* partakes less of narrated action and so much more of impression that more than one critic has compared Green's effects of light, color, and image to those of the Impressionist painters. What appears to be a brief description often becomes a study of objects in the light of a moment and then implies or, as noted before, symbolizes much more, as in the sexual symbolism of the dark mass of starlings swirling against a light sky. One striking example of Impressionist imagery out of many heralds the arrival of Mr. Rock and Elizabeth at the dance:

> A single pigeon, black in thickening sky,
> flew swift and on past the Park.
> It was dusk.
> Light from wide open windows increased by
> strides, primrose yellow over a dark that bled
> from blue.
> With a swoop an owl came down across and
> hooted while Mr. Rock and his daughter [*sic*]
> crept up the last stone flight. . . . (187)

This novel, especially, may be described more in terms of poetry than of prose fiction.

The main problem in *Concluding* as a novel is that of plot and action, but Green has done no differently in this respect, except in greater degree, than in previous novels, especially *Back* and *Party Going*. Many scenes are still slightly flickering in their sudden shifts and transitions, but they are not so much like the early movies as in *Living*. Nevertheless, most scenes contain little action. Characters look at the setting, which gives Green a frequent chance for description; and they talk quite a bit. But, though the events link to one another eventually, they involve less causal progression than a right and coherent plot would involve.

V   *More Circles*

The plot encompasses one day from predawn to nighttime, and the most important element of form, beyond the time of day, is a circular structure that is comparable to that of *Loving*. *Concluding* begins with Mr. Rock's prediction that "it will be a fine day" (5) and ends with the author's statement that, "on the whole [Rock] was well satisfied with his day" (254). Further supporting the circular form in *Concluding* are Mr. Rock's wandering pets. They are live creatures—a pig, a goose, a cat—rather than a dead peacock. Since there is no definite human agency involved, the loss and return of Mr. Rock's pets are less easily interpreted; but, besides their contributions to the mysterious atmosphere, they do clearly aid in the novel's continuity of events. The animals, all lost throughout the day, have returned at the end.

Throughout the novel an additional unifying element is the shouted call, "Mary!" The literal plot, however, is unfinished because Mary is never found; and Mr. Rock's status at the institute is not concretely settled. No flashback to important events of the previous night leads to events of the day and to a conclusion of a chain of events at the end. The plot remains incomplete in many ways, with unsolved mysteries and unresolved tensions, though unity of time and place provide a microcosm for Western civilization or at least England at a time when the state is trying to submerge the individual in the mass. Descriptions of the estate, as well as the actions of the characters, reveal what is being conveyed about the world and its future.

VI *Characters Real and Threatened*

In spite of the indeterminate nature of plot and setting, however, *Concluding* achieves novelistic exactitude in its major characterizations. The mysterious futuristic setting at a place somewhere within a short driving distance of London weaves several webs of meaning which would be broken if described in more specific terms. Most characters, except for the girls, are individualized. Throughout the work, Green stays with his purpose: those most threatend by the new mass society are the young; and many of these threats come from a state that is represented by older characters. Moreover, since some threats come from the older characters themselves, whether they realize it or not, the static again influences the dynamic; the old are influencing the young, not necessarily for good. Mr. Rock, the oldest person in the novel, is both recipient and agent of these patterns of influence.

Mr. Rock is, as his name implies, solid in his determination to protect what is his—his pets, his cottage, and his granddaughter. That he sometimes appears muddled or foolish can be attributed to his old age, to his deafness, or ultimately to his pride which is his strength. In the face of tribulation caused by the directors of the

institute and by the girls with their unfulfilled sexual urges, he retains
integrity and purity as few others do in the novel. Mr. Rock is for
stasis, however, where Misses Baker and Edge are for change; they
want him out of his cottage and off the estate. These ladies he can
combat with the innocence and cunning of the elderly. Less consciously, however, he victimizes the young. His granddaughter is his
chief care, but his solicitude inhibits her cure more than it helps. His
male presence stirs desires not only in the girls but also in Miss Edge
which, if satisfied, would corrupt as surely as old Adams does in the
woods at night, when, as the girls claim, they visit him for sexual
favors.

Full of hopes and fears, Rock stands firm through his most trying
day. He arises and goes to bed with optimism, and he encounters his
opponents and his fear of the darkness with the strength of a biblical
figure. In one of his few religious references, Green has Rock look at
the mansion looming in the moonlight "so tremendous that he spoke
out loud the name, 'Petra' " (245). The reference is reminiscent of the
play upon Greek words in Matthew 16:18 in which Christ says, "Thou
art Peter [*petros*—literally, 'a little rock'], and upon this rock [Petra] I
will build my church." This connection enhances Mr. Rock's strength
and dignity and implies triumph. He will not be driven from his
earthly paradise.

The chief antagonist in Mr. Rock's battle for the status quo is Miss
Mabel Edge, a co-directress of the institute with Miss Hermione
Baker. Though the two ladies are often described together as "those
two State parrots" (39) or as "a couple of old black herons" (219), they
are differentiated enough that one is never mistaken for the other. On
the surface, they are both conscious of directives from the state; but,
whereas Edge is more interested in the school, Baker weeps for "her"
orphans. Underneath their strong partnership, then, are some basic
antipathies. Miss Edge is herself in favor of the status quo; that is, she
wishes to maintain the estate and even return it to its former glory.
She loves the place. Baker, supporting state-ordered creation of a
black-and-white farm or—horror of horrors—pig farms, joins many
other Establishment characters whose names begin with *B*. Miss
Edge is on edge about her little world, and we recall that a rock can
either hone an edge or destroy it. An edge is active, whereas a rock
merely stands; but the edge may dash itself to destruction against the
rock.

The other members of the institute staff are sketched less clearly;
yet Green gives them differences. "Ma" Marchbanks worries about

the missing girls, and Maggie Blain rules her kitchen as a head cook should. Elizabeth, nearer the matrons' age than the girls', cannot adjust to pressures of state service, suffers a nervous breakdown, and reverts closer to the immature students. They rival her more for Sebastian Birt than does the teacher, Miss Winstanley, who also loves him. Elizabeth is partially released from her problem by sex when she is removed from direct state control from which the girls also are seeking release.

Sebastian Birt, besides being the only young man in the novel— younger than Elizabeth also—is set apart from the others by his not really knowing who he is. Sebastian is a surprising prophecy of the angry young man of the 1950s in his methods of escaping the state system, which are his sexual license and his role-playing mimicry. In his affectations of voice and facial expression, he is similar to Jim Dixon, Kingsley Amis's antihero in *Lucky Jim.*

The girls are rarely differentiated and then only briefly, sinking back into the mass later on. Merode stands out only as long as she is the returned runaway, for she is soon just another red-haired girl whose name begins with *M*. Otherwise all might be the same even as they rebel and seek natural freedom from the dehumanization of state control. Whether they win is never clearly answered, but nature and instinct are in their favor.

Concluding employs the most poetic technique of Green's novels and as such is impressive. By novelistic criteria, however, it must be judged less good than most of its predecessors, excluding *Blindness.* Green is most successful in *Concluding* in the difficult evocation of mystery and dream—almost to the extent of somnambulism— without losing touch with reality. He clearly reveals his continuing themes and dramatizes the possibility of depersonalization in a future Welfare State. With poetic elements such as imagery and symbolism—not allegory—Green deftly weaves a web of implications which the careful reader can detect.

In doing so, however, Green excludes attention to the traditional novelistic elements of plot and structure without which the novel is incomplete; it lacks a causally linked chain of actions and their conclusion. Though his implications provoke thought, they do not satisfy as a better-rounded plot usually does. Even more than *Back*, therefore, *Concluding* concludes not itself, but the integration of Green's novelistic techniques. In his last two novels, *Nothing* and *Doting*, the dangers inherent in his theory of narration through dialogue become evident.

CHAPTER 11

The Last Two

A FTER presenting the future in *Concluding*, Green returns to the portrayal of his own time in *Nothing* (1950) and in *Doting* (1952). Both novels are set in postwar England and follow *Back* chronologically. They also relate to *Back* because of more attention to human problems than to the sociopolitical implications of *Concluding*; yet both *Nothing* and *Doting* are by implication sociopolitical below the surface. These two works are set in the period of post–World War II reconstruction and austerity when the welfare state was beginning to level the new English generation. Moreover, working-class youths were beginning to have opportunities for occupations not open to them before, and upper-class youths were actually having to work for a living.

Nothing and *Doting* also are placed firmly within the Green canon by their link with the 1930s and with his novel of that decade, *Party Going*. Although Brendon Gill has even linked *Nothing* with many other novels of that decade, "witty and making no apology for their wit, light as air and assuming that air is as sound a measure of weight as lead,"[1] a consideration of this chronological relationship of *Nothing* and *Doting* with Green's earlier works is more substantial and informative. In fact, Green provides an unusual piece of internal evidence when he uses an incident from *Pack My Dag* in *Doting*. In the autobiographical *Pack My Bag*, he relates how outraged the girls at the party were when one young man told his dancing partner that her hair smelled good (226–27). Arthur Middleton, in *Doting*, relates this to the young Annabel Paynton as an incident from his own youth (32).

The parents in *Nothing* and *Doting*, therefore, could easily have been rich young British adults who attended parties in prewar France. After the war, they are just at the age to have children like those in both later novels who, born before the war, are almost the same age as the people of *Party Going*. The war, however, has done to their families' wealth what not even the Great Depression could do. Not only must the fathers work, but so must the younger generation—or it soon must do so. The younger characters, products of wartime drabness and of postwar austerity, work in civil service and take their jobs and lives far more soberly and seriously. They will not take the boat-train to a party in the South of France.

Green is not particularly complimentary about his own generation, but the characters representing it often turn out well or are at least more comfortable than we would expect. Many of Green's earlier apprehensions have come to pass, notably those suggested in *Party Going*; for, seen in the light of a more serious time, the shallowness of his generation is evident. Nevertheless, the soberness of the young generation is not necessarily an improvement; for, as an example, Mary Pomfret and Philip Weatherby in *Nothing* are, at their best, uninteresting as they exhibit their dreary propriety in contrast with their parents' remembered affairs and present social flightiness. In fact, these stodgy young lovers are interesting only as they search for their true parentage. Since Philip's mother and Mary's father once had an affair, they may be half-siblings. Who knows? Perhaps Philip's mother, but she laughingly does not say.

Annabel Paynton and Claire Belaine in *Doting* are sexually attractive to the older generation but less so to their own generation. Annabel complains that her young friend Terence Shone watches other boys too much; and another friend, Campbell Anthony, the poet, seems more preoccupied with a nebulous *weltschmerz* than with important matters like Annabel. Peter Middleton is enjoyable mostly because he is a typical schoolboy in Green's portrayal of his horrors, grumblings, and clumsiness. The younger generation in both novels, however, has lost a vitality with which the older characters still savor life, even if not in very admirable ways.

Nothing and *Doting* are thus in many ways similar. They reiterate many similar themes, situations, and techniques. Both, for instance, deal with the same themes found in Green's other novels as well as with the additional one of aging that is hinted at in the older characters of the earlier novels and presaged paradoxically in the futuristic *Concluding*. The sexual merry-go-round is similar in the situations of both novels, as is the rarefication of the author's techniques with dialogue. In this respect, the two novels are affected by Green's belief that a novelist should not tell the readers too much in order to be all things to all readers but should narrate almost exclusively by dialogue. Green always employs much dialogue, but he relieved it with poetically evocative descriptions until *Nothing* and *Doting*. These two comic novels have much to recommend interest; for, similar as they are, each differs enough from the other to require separate analysis. These differences are suggested by the themes that are indicated in their different titles, situations, characters, and descriptions.

I   Nothing *Is Something*

Nothing, when considered in its position in the Green canon, does arrive at something, though not so much richness of description, symbolism, and thematic content as previous novels. Green achieves a light, amusing wit mostly through dialogue; and, while dealing with his usual themes, he provides new characters and a still more recent setting than before (of course, with the exception of *Concluding*). *Nothing* reveals the loneliness of characters who seek relationships with their fellows—ones within their social circle, naturally. Jane Weatherby and John Pomfret, of the older generation, are widowed; and each is searching for new companionship, but the search is either frivolous or viciously comic. These sophisticated people are adept at feigning enthusiasm both about sex and about the bethrothal of their children, Philip and Mary; but Jane is masterfully vicious when she insures her own security by marrying John and by breaking Philip and Mary's engagement. Moreover, little Penelope Weatherby, who is as neurotic as a gushing but unloving mother can make her, is often Jane's foil for turning a troublesome conversation or situation to her advantage. Penelope's role is also to warn of the future, as did Miss Fellowes in *Party Going*, for she, even more than Philip and Mary, is suffering from the sins of her fathers. The characters, while delightfully shallow, are easily differentiated. They are intended to be typical of their time and their class rather than individuals; but, when they talk in Green's unerring conversational tones, they come alive individually.

One similarity with *Concluding* is that the older characters dominate *Nothing* rather than the younger. At any rate, Jane Weatherby becomes the major character as she manipulates the others like a female Machiavelli. Once again the static versus dynamic pattern develops as Jane and the older generation in general manage the younger generation and slyly tyrannize them. When Jane decides that she will discard Richard Abbot and marry John Pomfret, she must remove any threat that her son and John's daughter will marry; and she does so with grace. Even when she speaks to Mary in the hotel lobby at Brighton and Richard sneaks out behind Mary's back, Jane's poise is undisturbed. Kingsley Weatherhead has written that Jane knows whether John is Philip's true father, but she need not.[2] The main impediment which she sees to the children's marriage is that it would probably ruin her chances to snare John. Over numerous intimate little dinners she sets the trap; and John, who places comfort even before his daughter's happiness, is captured before he knows it. But their lives are changed very little.

John's mistress, Liz Jennings, and Jane's permanent escort, Richard Abbot, are unmarried hangers-on who gravitate to each other in their loneliness when cast adrift by the reunited couple. However, none of the older characters is lonelier than Arthur Morris, who lies in the hospital dying, literally, by inches. As he loses first a toe, then a leg, and finally his life, he recalls his friends'—Jane's and John's—past scandals for their children. Indeed, Philip and Mary, who seem to be his only visitors, are the loneliest characters in *Nothing*. They are victims of the older generation's nonchalant selfishness and of the developments in society, economics, and politics that have removed them from the moneyed and leisured class. In the world that their elders created, they must work in boring government bureaus in an atmosphere of serious triviality. They are, however, so solemnly stuffy, even during their courtship, that they do not elicit much sympathy, except when they are isolated from their families (Philip especially wished to be closer to his late father's family) and when they finally lose each other.

Love in this novel is something that also turns out to be nothing because it is false or forced or evolves as something else. Jane and John, for instance, have always been occupied with someone; but the variety of their partners may have been due to their desire for love or companionship. Conventional morality obviously has not been theirs, but they show in their actions of love much more vitality than their offspring. In the same manner, love for Richard and Liz is simply the seeking of attachments. Probably neither will ever marry even though they gravitate from John and Jane to each other. Richard's major emotional outlet is anger at waiters to the point of apoplexy while Liz, if not "the drunk" which gossip labels her to be, is at least an aging mistress. Neither is portrayed as having much depth of feeling.

The shallow older generation's view of love is made clear in its effect on the younger generation. If the older generation goes through the motions of love, no matter with what enthusiasm, the younger generation does not even do that. The reader is as surprised as Jane and John when Philip announces his engagement to Mary at his twenty-first birthday party, for their tepid conversations over "Dutch" lunches have taken their courtship amazingly far toward marriage. They are attuned to the lower-class attitude that they might as well get married since they lack anything better to do. Twenty-five years before, their parents had bounced into bed, had enjoyed themselves, and had then gone their separate ways.

There may be neurosis in the courtship propriety of Philip and Mary, but Jane denies that Philip's sexual urges are abnormal. In spite of his promise to his mother that he will discuss everything with her first, Philip is repressed rather than perverted. Penelope, Philip's little, neurotic sister, has taken the mock marriage ceremony with John seriously, if we are to believe Jane's story of Penelope's behavior. Jane, however, gives the impression that her voluble concern about "the little saint" is a way of covering her unconcern. Love here is reduced, if not to nothingness, at least to externals with everyone merely going through the motions.

Social dissolution is reflected in *Nothing* by the remnants of Green's own class. Rather than love, society is the dominant concern of this novel as it portrays the comic emptiness of a decaying upper middle class. The times that Green traces contain many events of sufficient magnitude to cause such changes—depression, world war, and postwar economic problems. Many members of the prewar moneyed set find themselves working to pay astronomical taxes or economizing to live off inherited income. Besides the drastic reduction in parties and dances, this social group has to cope with more "singles"—people widowed, divorced, or never married because of wartime emergency.

Times have changed, but the generation that helped create and then fought the war continues to think, if not to live, in the past. This generation's children, who will inherit the society they have not affected, are victims of a sort of emotional death. Although Philip and Mary seek secure identity in old family ties and in older conventional behavior, their parents are uncomprehending because they never held these older values. The old employees of hotels and restaurants recall richer days when the older generation was young and was spending fortunes on entertainment, but Jane has to pawn her brooch to finance Philip's twenty-first birthday party. Caterers Pascal and Gaspard outdo themselves to supply magnificent decor and food not only for old times' sake, but also because they no longer have much

III   *From* Loving *to* Doting

But, in spite of similarity to the preceding novel, *Doting* shows chronological advancement; for the title suggests passage from early middle age to late middle age, the very brink of old age. Though individual characters dote on one another, they imply that society in general has reached this dotage. Although Green continues the themes which have run almost unbroken throughout his other novels, human loneliness plays less of a part here than previously; for most of the characters in *Doting* have companions, and no one feels very deeply about his condition. Arthur Middleton reaches an early dotage involving bored young ladies; and the widower, Charles Addinsell, is later drawn into the intrigues using his sad story about the loss of his wife, Penelope, to attract girls to his bedroom. Younger ones, such as Annabel and Claire, are seeking attachment or are growing to the time when they must seek it, like Peter. Although his characters are sometimes alone or depressed, Green depicts the humor in their situation, not claustrophobic isolation.

Sex figures in *Doting* even more than in *Nothing*, though *Nothing* contains more instances of successful extramarital sex. Arthur and Diana Middleton are married, as John Pomfret and Jane Weatherby are not. Arthur tries a last fling in his attempt to seduce young Annabel Paynton, but he fails, just as widower Charles Addinsell does in his pursuit of Diana and Annabel. Charles finally succeeds with Annabel's friend, Claire Belaine, and his is the novel's only such success. Campbell Anthony and Terence Shone are too young, Annabel complains, but she returns to them in the end. Both Diana and Arthur try to get Diana's Charles interested in Arthur's young girls in order to preserve their own marriage, but this trickery backfires on both of them: Arthur is still stuck with a cooling Annabel, and Diana is left without an extramarital male admirer and confidante.

The same impression of social dissolution is made in *Doting* as in *Nothing* by the characters who are members of Green's own social class. The older men, Arthur and Charles, work much harder for less income than before World War II; and, whereas Annabel and Claire would have been debutantes before, they are now working girls which, Green implies, makes them more openly predatory. Before the war, they would have attended balls and house parties where they could meet eligible young men; they now work all day; they have nowhere to go at night unless invited out by older men with some money to spare;[3] and the young men their age cannot afford to entertain them. Drab nightclubs provide the few opportunities for social life, and business lunches are associated with clandestine courtship. As Nanny Swift in Green's *Loving* foretold, the upper classes are experiencing some changes.

The characters are so set in their expectable roles that they are almost types, but they talk themselves into revealing marvelous human differences precisely because they have so little of moment to do, and do it with such empty-headed vitality. As in *Nothing*, the middle-aged couple, the oldest characters in the novel, dominate the situation; and Arthur Middleton (for "middle age"?) is the most active in his persistent attempts to sow a middle-aged crop of wild oats with young Annabel. He protests so seriously to his friend Charles Addinsell that he is enamored of Annabel that we wonder briefly whether he does not mean it; but, of course, he is only doting. Diana, Arthur's wife and the mother who defends her home from the attractions that youth has for middle age, talks a mile a minute and manipulates everyone up to a point, including her friend Charles; but she is not so Machiavellian as her predecessor, Jane Weatherby. Though Diana's ego receives the necessary lift, she fends off Charles's seduction attempts. She knows that the marriage bed is still her best weapon in the battle of the sexes; and that bed, as V. S. Pritchett has noted, becomes, if not a central object in the novel, at least ubiquitous.[4]

The Middleton's son Peter, though only a minor character, is also portrayed three dimensionally. His adolescent horror at the thought of Annabel's dating an upperclassman at his school, his yells of starvation when the food service is slow, and his other gaucheries contribute to a clearly portrayed character. One of the few bits of growth in any of these lives is shown when he graduates from drinking shandy at the beginning of the novel to sneaking sips of champagne at the end of it. The next barrier to fall will be his rejection of the frivolous exercise grown-ups call dancing.

Annabel, who uses an expiring voice for romantic telephone conversations and for crucial face-to-face encounters, is a clever little schemer who wants a good time in spite of her reduced station in life. In England's Age of Austerity, she and Claire must be ready for "the main chance" if they are to go out with men for any fun at all. Cautious Annabel's plots come to very little, but Claire, who is slyer and more desperate, takes Charles away from Annabel simply by going to bed with him. In Green's best ironic touch in the novel, the horrified

Annabel and Diana reject the sinful couple. Both girls, however, are resilient because Diana retains her husband and Annabel can always return to Campbell or even young Terence.

Charles Addinsell plays all games and forms a convenient pivot on the sexual seesaw. The Middletons' long-standing agreement that one could go out alone with a friend if the other is not invited tempts Charles to make a play for Diana. She is interested only in being reassured about her continued desirability, however, so he tries his lugubrious technique first on Annabel and then on Claire. Poor Penelope, his late wife, died so young that he is afraid to remarry, afraid that he will be left alone again; but he does need some tenderness and the right kind of sympathy to cheer him.

As we have noted, few of these characters ever love; they dote. (*Love* is rarely used and *dote* appears repeatedly.) Doting is the *reductio ad absurdum* of loving, and the two novels, *Loving* and *Doting*, stand in just such a relationship. In both novels, characters are reaching out for love, at least as far as they understand the emotion; and Green mentions most forms of physical and emotional relationships. Both novels also are conveyed in humorous terms. As V. S. Pritchett has observed, "The comedy begins when doting leads to cross-doting, when the partners of the comedy of manners change and rechange."[5]

The process of changing and rechanging leads characters in a circle, shallow and doting, but the implication is that this life continues always in much the same way since no one feels any emotion very strongly. Diana seeks to preserve a comfortable marriage both for occasional sex and for her son, but her nagging and small talk are as strong as any intentional forces she brings to bear on the problem. Arthur dotes on Annabel in a way different from but as shallow as Diana's feelings. Charles dotes on young ladies who fall for his "line" about poor Penelope. Annabel does not like the way Terence dotes on other boys. Doting, the leitmotif in the novel, shows everyone's debilitation; if life is middle-aged for the older characters, society is for the younger.

With almost as much dialogue as in the previous novel, most of the narration is done obliquely through the characters' conversations. As in *Nothing*, Green provides little description and few symbols or images; instead, he repeats his attempts to rely on dialogue and a few stage directions to develop a novel.[6] The conversation, still sharp and true-to-life, is full of innuendo, repetition, and obliquity, especially with Arthur and Diana, who have been married almost two decades.

As married couples will, they communicate by references and implications that refer to mutual experiences. Diana interrupts a serious
conversation to tell her husband that their son has caught his first
salmon; then, after conventional but strained enthusiasm from Arthur, they go to bed. When Diana protests, "But I saw your hand!"
she refers to the compromising scene of Arthur's dabbling at the
coffee stains on the skirtless Annabel. This refrain is repeated at
crucial moments, such as those when Diana is losing to Arthur's logic,
until it virtually becomes a leitmotif like E. M. Forster's "only
connect. . . ." But Green is capable of appropriate variety so that the
girl talk between Annabel and Claire or the man talk between Arthur
and Charles has the ring of everyday conversation.

IV *The Old Green*

As in *Nothing*, *Doting* has few true descriptions like the earlier
novels; but at least three provide information which could appear in
no other way. As the novel opens, the main characters, Annabel,
Peter, and his parents, are in a nightclub where a juggler performs.
We notice that this entertainer acts with the indifference of the
characters; but at the end, in a different nightclub, when the same
juggler appears, we feel that Green has inserted the scenes to show
that life is artifice. In other words, objects are invested with meaning
in this otherwise bare novel about devious characters who lead
empty, unperceptive lives in the same old circles. Just as the juggler
in nightclubs at the beginning and the end first balances objects on his
chin and then throws balls up in an ever enlarging circle, the love
affairs and their necessary machinations move in circles through the
novel.

Green, however, also describes the juggler as "the artist" (the tarot
juggler means creativity), but the characters see only sleight-of-hand
(10). This artificiality is reinforced by the other nightclub performers,
such as the exotic dancer who charms a basket of fake snakes and the
wrestlers, who often perform to a prearranged plot but who do not
even appear. The characters' futile lives are revealed when they see
fakery rather than creativity. Again, the hilarious scene when Arthur
has Annabel for a cozy dinner while his wife and son are gone could
only have been described by a narrator. Arthur, as he makes a pass at
Annabel, spills coffee on her skirt; she whips it off to save it; and in
walks Diana. When Green fortunately violated his theory a trifle

more in *Doting* than in *Nothing* to provide these scenes, a touch of the old Green reappeared.

An interesting aspect of Green's title and its similarity to *Loving* is the slight rise, again, in symbolism and imagery that relates primarily to doting, juggling, and the circular nature of life and that make for greater interest than anything *Nothing* evokes. All of the characters except the inarticulate schoolboy Peter dote on someone else—and often on more than one. Arthur, for instance, says, "I love you" to Annabel (165), but he had earlier explained the difference between loving and doting by saying that "loving goes deeper" (50). To complete the fun that Green has with his title, he also allows the melancholy young poet, Campbell Anthony, as Annabel tells Arthur, to work on "an anthology of love poetry he's to call 'Doting' " (50). Green has never before shown his theme either so obviously or so skillfully, except in *Back* where the repeated word "rose" not only is thematically related to Charley Summer's fall and rebirth but is also emblematic of his mental instability.

None of Green's birds flies in *Doting*, but Peter carries a dead goose back to school. The foolishness of the characters' lives is obviously implied by the goose, especially as a schoolboy appears with it on a railway platform. More subtly, however, since it is mentioned on the first page as something that will happen after the book has ended, the scene with the goose helps form another silly circle in the pattern of these characters' lives.

The plot, though light, is shapely because, as we have noted, of the circular pattern Green enjoys. The scenes still contain at least two persons because of the necessity for dialogue but, like movie scenes, remain clear-cut. They form a circle as the married couple, Arthur and Diana, go off toward extramarital adventures and then return. Annabel goes from her interest in young men almost into a liaison with an older man and then back to the young. Her friend Claire comes nearer to violating the circle with Charles, but she is not so attractive as Annabel. Also, that little affair is not quite over at the novel's end; but the last sentence, "The next day they all went on very much the same," implies that their relationship will end as the others did.

Doting, then, is similar to *Nothing* in narrative technique, theme, and subject matter. They are not bad novels; they are humorous; they are thematically meaningful. And they are readable, for Green is generally successful at narrative through dialogue. His theory of

fictional technique, however, is aimed in an unsatisfactory direction
because the exclusive use of dialogue cannot supply all the demands
upon a novel. Green's novels lack the quality of his earlier works
because of the reduced amount of descriptive imagery and symbolism; and, though character, plot, and theme are realized, the
characters are shallow, and the plots are uneventful.

CHAPTER 12

Drawing Conclusions

F ROM the publication of *Doting* in 1952 until his death in 1973 Green produced no novel. In spite of his problems with the creation of fiction, especially after his retirement from business in 1958, Green was considered to be in a fallow period between novels as he was from 1926 to 1929, from 1929 to 1939, and again from 1940 to 1943. He had reasons for these earlier breaks; between *Blindness* and *Living*, for instance, he began "Mood," which he did not finish. Between *Living* and *Party Going*, he was busy with his other occupation; and, after *Pack My Bag*, the beginning of World War II prevented his quick return to novel publication. This period after *Doting*, however, was too long; for in 1957, after he responded to the request that he write a book about firefighting in the London Blitz, only portions of this work were published, according to John Russell, in the *London Magazine* and in the *Texas Quarterly*.[1] That these excerpts are all that appeared in print is regrettable since Green returned in these segments to rich narrative and descriptive prose after the bare dialogue of *Nothing* and *Doting*.

Reflections of the old Green of *Caught* and *Loving* in his projected "London and Fire, 1940," include his oblique approach to the subject of World War II by way of Cork, Ireland, in 1938. He also retains some of his old flavor in realistic dialogue when he recreates mothers' complaints at the beginning of the war about the absence of gasmasks for infants: "What use is this [gasmask] to me if poor Ernie ain't got nothing?" and "Then what do you suggest I do with sweet Peter here, poor little mite?"[2]

Green provides excellent background for *Caught* with his descriptions of the London Fire Brigade, "not so much huge as squat and broad with spade-like faces,"[3] and with his listing of supplies called in for the coming war. Anecdotes are rich as when "a fireman took the hook ladder off his D. P., 'scaled,' as they say, the unscathed building, put the ladder across a wall between the two, crossed over,

137

went down and fetched those girls up, then led them across his bridge to love, life, and laughter."[4] From the soft-spoken superintendent to the brigade members who burned their "wet canteen" to destroy their overdue beer bills, Green portrays all the regulars who served as instructors for the Auxiliary Fire Service. Material in this single article suggests several novels, including one on the London slum children who were evacuated to country homes and who had their first experience with peas that were not from a can or milk not from a bottle. Mrs. Welch's Albert in *Loving* is a brief example.

If his memories of the Blitz and firefighting are vivid to his readers, they are more vivid to Green; and such recall may be one reason why he was unable to finish the book. That the traumas of World War II were still strong in Green is emphasized by his second attempt at a book since *Doting*. In a sequel of sorts to *Pack My Bag*, he came to the period 1939–1945, but he could not write about it. Instead, he thought of bridging it with a sentence saying that enough has been written about that period already and that he would skip over it.[5] Also after retirement, he became, if anything, more private, even reclusive, than before.[6] He had, in effect, taken himself out of circulation; and this retreat may have weakened his knack for envisioning and creating characters.

I   *End of a Novel Theory*

The accomplishment of his theory about the novel in *Nothing* and in *Doting* did not help with his subsequent writing. The belief that a novel should be all things to all men by reducing description to stage directions and by narrating through dialogue removed some valuable richness from his work, but it emphasized another of his strong points, realistic conversation. More troublesome is the fact that he repeated himself; *Doting* is too much like *Nothing*, and it signals no artistic advancement over his past career. Perhaps no further advancement was possible.

Even if Green added no more to his canon, his work is a solid achievement. His canon demonstrates a unity of theme and a high level of artistic development. While always recognizably his own, each novel, except *Doting*, has surprising differences in setting and situation from the one before. He always brings his individual perceptions to portrayals of human life by selecting, synthesizing, and generalizing to reach a universal meaning. In spite of this artistic role, his oblique approach keeps him from exposing himself to the reader in even his most personal situation, especially the harrowing experiences of World War II that are seen in *Caught*.

The most convincing unity is found in his consistent development of major themes. From *Blindness* to *Doting*, Green portrays human loneliness in almost as many situations as he has characters. The answer to this human loneliness is almost always love, but Green does not provide solutions for everyone. Lily Gates, for example, loses the man she chooses first. The optimism of Green's novels is found not in characters' achieving a solution for loneliness but in their continuing quest for the solution. But the most striking of Green's themes is social and economic change. Gradually, as he has foreseen and portrayed, the upper classes have lost control of their world to the working classes. These changes have been painful for everyone; both Richard Dupret (upper class) and Lily Gates (lower class) in *Living* are frustrated in their desires. Overlooking the prophetic warning in *Party Going*, there is not a clear shift until *Loving* in the balance toward the servants like Raunce and away from the owner, Mrs. Tennant. *Concluding* reveals the prophetic leap into the future welfare state ruled by the workers, and this futuristic glimpse underscores the fact depicted in *Nothing* and *Doting* that the former leisure class must now work.

Green's technical virtuosity does not limit his appeal to many readers, for his themes are universal problems that fit his own times almost to the degree of being prophetic. Admitting a decline of inspiration in his last two novels, we still must credit his achievement—the mixture of poetry and realism which he balanced best in *Living* and *Loving* but maintained in a fascinating manner from *Party Going* to *Concluding*. The psychological tensions of *Caught* and *Back* are increasingly impressive, and even *Nothing* and *Doting* are still amusing.

II *The Prose Stylist*

How Green wrote, however, is often more impressive than what he wrote. His style has a poetic richness that enhances the significance of everyday objects and discloses the mystery inherent in anything man encounters in life. At times, Green imbues something animate or inanimate with symbolic import; but he is not, strictly speaking, a British Kafka like Rex Warner, author of *Aerodrome*, who admits the Kafkaesque influence, which Green does not. Green uses flowers, especially roses; colors, especially those of fire; and animals, especially birds—all kinds of birds from pigeons to peacocks—to enrich the appearance and the meaning of the world he creates. As in life, however, so it is with Green's symbolism—things can be sublime at one moment and mundane at another. Nevertheless, when Green uses an object as a symbol—taking diversionary references out of account—his meaning is consistent and not vascillating.

As an original prose stylist, Green stands as alone among British writers as did the American genius William Faulkner, whom he admired. Perceptive readers of all types have enjoyed the richness of his descriptions. At his most unsuccessfully flowery, his descriptive passages never reach the lush exaggeration of Lawrence Durrell's least successful poetic prose in the *Alexandria Quartet*. When Green is humorous, as in *Loving* or *Doting*, he strikes the popular funny bone, especially the scene in which Arthur, in midseduction, knocks the coffee onto Annabel's skirt. Green always felt free to seek the appropriate style for each occasion, and even his titles continue to amuse and fascinate readers as "deadpan approximations to an anti-rhetorical world of linguistic analysis."[7]

Green, who is consistently successful in the recreation of dialogue, reproduces conversation with an unerring sense of the true rhythms of English talk. The commonplace and the cliché contribute to reality rather than to monotony. Repetition occurs as people actually repeat themselves in conversation, and Green's characters often fail to communicate just as other people do. In this respect, he approaches the style of Chekhov—or Laurence Sterne in the hobbyhorse theory of conversation: each person talks in terms of his own consuming passion instead of answering the other. As a result, dialogue has been a powerful element in Green's characterizations. Though he peoples the novels with recognizable types and classes, the types and classes from Cockney to the very rich live and move and talk as they do in the works of few other modern novelists. He knows the people about whom he writes because he has met and observed them or their counterparts. If Mr. Rock is a projection of Green's old age, he has even used himself as a latter-day source.

III *Reception and Influence*

Green achieved critical acclaim, but he never received status on the best-seller lists. Most of his works remain in print, and most of the critical estimates of his literary achievements remain positive, but some are absolutely ecstatic. He has been commended by fellow writers from Philip Toynbee to Eudora Welty as having had the most imaginative talent and as being the best novelist of the present age. Although other critics temper the estimate to that of a minor novelist, he is placed in the first rank in that category by Martin Greenberg or is considered a minor novelist with several excellent qualities by Isaac Rosenfeld. When there is completely adverse criticism, it usually involves individual novels, especially the last two; his novel theory (C. P. Snow); or his personal eccentricities such as his insistence upon pseudonymity or his aversion to being photographed. But, even in these cases, he has never lacked defenders.

The excuse that we either like Green's work very much or not at all is probably too much of a cliché. Still, he is so original and imaginative that readers feel impelled to make some personal estimate. An impressive aspect of these personal estimates is that many of the critics are, themselves, literary figures. W. H. Auden wrote enthusiastically about Green, whose work admittedly includes elements of poetry. John Updike, a vocal American disciple, says that *Loving* will be one of tomorrow's classics.[8] Green's critical reputation for abstruseness, for sophistication, and for the frequency with which he has been reviewed by other literary artists identify him as a writer's writer even if he is not a popular novelist.

For a novelist who did not publish a novel after 1952, Green continues to excite critical attention. Articles continue to appear not only in the United States and in Great Britain but also on the European Continent from France to the Balkans. His acceptance in academic circles increases as critiques are published by professors and as dissertations are written (at least five from 1970 to 1977) by their students. Old friends in England like John Lehmann agree with Paul Bailey, who maintains that Green "deserves greater recognition."[9]

Green's importance as a novelist continues and his fame increases. He need not be widely influential, though Terry Southern acknowledges his debt to Green's work, especially in *Flash and Filigree*.[10] While Green is not revolutionary, he is refreshingly independent and original; but how near he is to greatness remains debatable. Regrettably, he did not turn that next corner, as many novelists do in the evolution of their writing theories and techniques, which would have assured him of continued development and which he did each time before *Doting*. Instead, recognizing the limitations of his novelistic theory—and perhaps of his inspiration—he accepted the wisdom of quitting while he was ahead and stopped in a theoretical *cul-de-sac*.

Notes and References

Books by Henry Green are cited parenthetically in the text. See the Selected Bibliography for editions used.

Chapter One

1. Autobiographical sketch, *New York Herald Tribune Book Review*, October 8, 1950, p. 14.
2. Nigel Dennis, "The Double Life of Henry Green," *Life*, XXXIII (August 4, 1952), p. 84.
3. Edward Stokes, *The Novels of Henry Green* (London, 1959), p. 23.
4. "A Novelist to His Readers," *The Listener*, XLIV (November 9, 1950), p. 506.
5. Anthony Quinton, "A French View of *Loving*," *The London Magazine*, VI (April 1959), p. 34.
6. Philip Toynbee, "The Novels of Henry Green," *Partisan Review*, XVI (May 1949), p. 494.
7. V. S. Pritchett, "Green on Doting," *The New Yorker*, XXVIII (May 17, 1952), p. 139.
8. James Hilton, "Two More by Mr. Green," *New York Herald Tribune Book Review* (December 31, 1950), p. 4.
9. Stokes, *op. cit.*
10. *Ibid.*
11. On Green in *Blindness*, for example, see D. W. Brogan, "Recent Fiction," *The New Republic*, XLIX (December 29, 1926), p. 174. For Roe as a self-projection of Green in *Caught*, see Bruce Bain, "Henry Green: The Man and His Work," *World Review*, No. 3 (May 1949), p. 57.
12. Terry Southern, "The Art of Fiction XXII: Henry Green," *The Paris Review*, V (Summer 1958), p. 65.
13. Stokes, *op. cit.*, pp. 133, 18.
14. A. Kingsley Weatherhead, *A Reading of Henry Green* (Seattle, 1961), p. 144.

Chapter Two

1. Quoted by Nigel Dennis, *op. cit.*, p. 84.
2. See a discussion of "non-representational" by Donald S. Taylor, "Catalytic Rhetoric: Henry Green's Theory of the Modern Novel," *Criticism*, VII (Winter 1965), p. 82.
3. "The English Novel of the Future," *Contact*, I (August 1950), p. 22.

4. C. P. Snow, "Books and Writers," *The Spectator*, CLXXXV (September 22, 1950), p. 320.

5. Alan Ross, "Green, with Envy: Critical Reflections and an Interview," *The London Magazine*, VI (April 1959), p. 24.

6. "Novel of the Future," p. 22.

7. "A Fire, a Flood, and the Price of Meat," *The Listener*, XLVI (August 23, 1951), p. 294.

8. "A Novelist to His Readers," *The Listener*, XLIV (November 9, 1950), pp. 505–506.

9. For discussions of Green's humor see Taylor, *op. cit.*, pp. 84–85, and Bruce Johnson, "Henry Green's Comic Symbolism," *Ball State University Forum*, VI (Autumn 1965), pp. 29–35.

10. Terry Southern, "The Art of Fiction XXII: Henry Green," *The Paris Review*, V (Summer 1958), pp. 67–68.

11. "Novel of the Future," p. 23.

12. *Ibid.*, p. 21.

13. "A Novelist to His Readers—II," *The Listener*, XLV (March 15, 1951), p. 425.

14. "Novel of the Future," p. 23, and Southern, "The Art of Fiction," pp. 66–67.

15. "A Novelist," p. 505.

16. "The Spoken Word as Written," *The Spectator*. CXCI (September 4, 1953), p. 248.

17. *Ibid.*

18. *Ibid.*

19. Giorgio Melchiori, *The Tightrope Walkers* (London, 1956), p. 195.

20. "Novel of the Future," p. 23.

21. Southern, "The Art of Fiction," p. 66.

22. "Novel of the Future," p. 23.

23. "A Novelist," p. 506.

24. Philip Toynbee, "The Novels of Henry Green," *Partisan Review*, XVI (May 1949), p. 489.

25. Ross, *op. cit.*, p. 23.

26. "Apologia," *Folios of New Writing*, IV (Autumn 1941), p. 49.

27. "Novel of the Future," p. 22.

28. For example, C. M. Bowra, *Memories 1898–1939* (London, 1967), p. 163.

29. William York Tindall, *The Literary Symbol* (Bloomington, 1955), p. 97.

30. Walter Allen, "An Artist of the Thirties," *Folios of New Writing*, III (Spring 1941), p. 154.

31. Southern, "The Art of Fiction," p. 75.

32. Robert L. Weaver, "The Novels of Henry Green," *The Canadian Forum*, XXX (January 1951), p. 230.

33. Melchiori, *op. cit.*, p. 193.

Chapter Three

1. "Edward Garnett," *New Statesman and Nation*, XL n.s. (December 30, 1950), p. 675.

2. D. W. Brogan, *op. cit.*, p. 174, and Anon., "The New Books" (rev. of *Blindness*), *Saturday Review of Literature*, III (December 25, 1926), p. 472.

3. Anon., "The New Books."

4. Walter Allen, "Henry Green," *The Penguin New Writing*, No. 25 (1945), p. 147.

5. Rupert Brooke, *The Poetical Works of Rupert Brooke*, ed. Geoffrey Keynes, 2nd ed. (London: Faber and Faber Limited, 1970), p. 35.

6. John Russell, "There It Is," *The Kenyon Review*, XXVI (Summer 1964), p. 444.

7. John Russell, *Henry Green: Nine Novels and an Unpacked Bag* (New Brunswick, New Jersey, 1960), pp. 67–68.

8. Terry Southern, "The Art of Fiction XXII: Henry Green," *The Paris Review*, V (Summer 1958), p. 73.

9. Russell, *Henry Green*, p. 67.

10. "An Unfinished Novel," *The London Magazine*, VI (April 1959), p. 12.

11. *Ibid.*, p. 17.

Chapter Four

1. Walter Allen, *The Modern Novel in Britain and the United States* (New York, 1964), p. 214.

2. Anon., "The Bookman's Diary," *The Bookman* (London), LXXVI (June 1929), p. 168.

3. Edward Stokes, *op. cit.*, p. 101.

4. See James Hall, *The Tragic Comedians: Seven Modern British Novelists* (Bloomington, 1963), pp. 66–67.

5. Stokes, *op. cit.*, p. 101.

6. R. M. Linscott, "Cinematograph," *New York Herald Tribune Book Review*, August 11, 1929, p. 2.

Chapter Five

1. Ruth Chapin, "Green Posturing," *Christian Science Monitor*, September 13, 1951, p. 11.

2. Robert L. Weaver, *op. cit.*, p. 228.

3. I am not saying here that this novel is a poem as did Anthony Burgess in *The Novel Now* (New York, 1957), p. 111.

4. A. Kingsley Weatherhead, *A Reading of Henry Green* (Seattle, 1961), p. 52.

5. Discussion of this quotation as a prose rather than a poetic technique is found in Bruce Bassoff, "Prose Consciousness in the Novels of Henry Green," *Language and Style*, V (1972), pp. 276–77.

Chapter Six

1. Max Cosman, "The Elusive Henry Green," *Commonweal*, LXXII (September 9, 1960), p. 472.

2. See, for example, Philip Toynbee, "New Novels," *The New Statesman and Nation*, XXV (June 26, 1943), p. 422, and "The Novels of Henry Green," *Partisan Review*, XVI (May 1949), p. 492.

3. John Russell, *Henry Green: Nine Novels and an Unpacked Bag* (New Brunswick, New Jersey, 1960), p. 8.

4. "A Private School in 1914," *Folios of New Writing* (Spring 1940), pp. 11–25.

Chapter Seven

1. John Lehmann, *I Am My Brother* (New York, 1960), p. 109.

2. "A Rescue," *The Penguin New Writing* (March 1941), p. 93.

3. "Mr. Jonas," *The Penguin New Writing* (September 1942), p. 20.

4. Walter Allen, "Henry Green," *The Penguin New Writing* (1945), pp. 144–55, and "Greening," *New Statesman*, LVII (May 2, 1959), pp. 615–16.

5. "The Lull," *New Writing and Daylight* (Summer 1943), pp. 11–21.

Chapter Eight

1. John Russell, "There It Is," *The Kenyon Review*, XXVI (Summer 1964), pp. 450–51.

2. Giorgio Melchiori, *op. cit.*, p. 211.

3. Edward Stokes, *op. cit.*, p. 163.

4. William York Tindall, *op. cit.*, p. 97.

5. Ernest Jones, "The Double View," *The Nation*, CLXIX (October 22, 1949), p. 402.

6. Theodore Kalem, "Green: Ironist of the Human Heart," *Christian Science Monitor*, October 27, 1949, p. 11.

Chapter Nine

1. John Russell, "There It Is," *The Kenyon Review*, XXVI (Summer 1964), pp. 438–39.

2. Orville Prescott, *In My Opinion: An Inquiry Into the Contemporary Novel* (Indianapolis, 1952), p. 97.

3. Stephen A. Shapiro, "Henry Green's *Back*: The Presence of the Past," *Critique: Studies in Modern Fiction*, VII (Spring 1964), p. 90.

Chapter Ten

1. Edward Stokes, *op. cit.*, p. 170.

2. James Hall, *op. cit.*, p. 78.

3. See also A. Kingsley Weatherhead, "Structure and Texture in Henry Green's Latest Novels," *Accent*, XIX (Spring 1959), p. 112.

4. Robert L. Weaver, *op. cit.*, p. 230.

5. For example, Stokes, *op. cit.*, p. 177.

6. *Ibid.*, pp. 19–20.

7. *Ibid.*, p. 175.

Chapter Eleven

1. Brendon Gill, "Something," *The New Yorker*, XXVI (March 25, 1950), p. 103.

2. A. Kingsley Weatherhead, *A Reading of Henry Green* (Seattle, 1961), p. 124.

3. J. D. Scott, "New Novels," *New Statesmen and Nation*, XLIII (May 10, 1952), pp. 564, 566.

4. V. S. Pritchett, *op. cit.*, p. 137.

5. *Ibid.*

6. See also Norman Page, *Speech in the Novel* (London, 1973), pp. 129–32.

Chapter Twelve

1. John Russell, "There It Is," *The Kenyon Review*, XXVI (Summer 1964), p. 450.

2. "Firefighting," *The Texas Quarterly*, III (Winter 1960), p. 106.

3. *Ibid.*, p. 111.

4. *Ibid.*, p. 110.

5. Russell, "There It Is," p. 451.

6. John Lehmann, Personal Interview, Austin, Texas, May 10, 1971.

7. John Hollander, *Vision and Resonance: Two Senses of Poetic Form* (New York, 1975), p. 225.

8. John Updike in "Tomorrow's Classics," *Avant Garde*, No. 6 (January 1969), p. 28. For a longer appreciation of Green by Updike see "A Comment," *The Times Literary Supplement*, No. 3,249 (June 4, 1964), p. 473.

9. Paul Bailey, "This Is Henry Green—He Deserves Greater Recognition," *Nova* (September 1969), pp. 22, 27, 30, 33.

10. Terry Southern, Personal Letter, September 18, 1975.

Selected Bibliography

PRIMARY SOURCES
(in order of first publication)

Blindness. London: J. M. Dent and Sons Ltd., 1926.*New York: E. P. Dutton and Co., Inc., 1926.

Living. London: Hogarth Press, 1929.* New York: E. P. Dutton and Co., Inc., 1929.

Party Going. London: Hogarth Press, 1939. New York: Viking Press, 1951.*

"A Private School in 1914." *Folios of New Writing.* I (Spring 1940), 11–25.

Pack My Bag. London: Hogarth Press, 1940.

"A Rescue." *Penguin New Writing* (March 1941), 88–93.

"Mr. Jonas." *Folios of New Writing.* III (Spring 1941), 11–17. *Penguin New Writing* (September 1942), 15–20.* *Diversion,* edited by Hester W. Chapman and Princess Romanovsky-Pavlovsky. London: Collins, 1946.

"Apologia." *Folios of New Writing.* IV (Autumn 1941), 44–51.

Caught. London: Hogarth Press, 1943. New York: Viking Press, 1952.*

"The Lull." *New Writing and Daylight* (Summer 1943), 11–21.

Loving. London: Hogarth Press, 1945. New York: Viking Press, 1949.*

Back. London: Hogarth Press, 1946.* New York: Viking Press, 1950.

Concluding. London: Hogarth Press, 1948. New York: Viking Press, 1950.*

Nothing. London: Hogarth Press, 1950. New York: Viking Press, 1950.*

"The English Novel of the Future." *Contact.* I (August 1950), 21–24.

Autobiographical Sketch. *New York Herald Tribune Book Review.* October 8, 1950, 14.

"A Novelist to His Readers." *The Listener.* LXIV (November 9, 1950), 505–506.

"Edward Garnett." *New Statesman and Nation.* XL n.s. (December 30, 1950), 675.

"A Novelist to His Readers—II." *The Listener.* XLV (March 15, 1951), 425, 427.

"A Fire, a Flood, and the Price of Meat." *The Listener*, XLVI (August 23, 1951), 293–94.

Doting. London: Hogarth Press, 1952. New York: Viking Press, 1952.*

"The Spoken Word as Written," review of *The Oxford Book of English Talk. Spectator.* CXCI (September 4, 1953), 248.

*Where more than one edition is listed, this edition is the one cited in the text.

148

Review of Virginia Woolf's *A Writer's Diary*. *London Magazine*. I (February 1954), 80–83.

"An Unfinished Novel." *London Magazine*. VI (April 1959), 11–17.

"Firefighting." *The Texas Quarterly*. III (Winter 1960), 105–20.

"For Jenny with Affection from Henry Green." *Spectator*. CCXI (October 4, 1963), 422.

1. Original Materials

LEHMANN, JOHN. Personal Interview on Henry Green and his works. Austin, Texas, May 10, 1971.

SOUTHERN, TERRY. Personal Letter referring to Henry Green's influence on Southern's writing. September 18, 1975.

YORKE, MRS. HENRY V. Personal Interview on Henry Green and his works in his home. London, England, July 5, 1976.

SECONDARY SOURCES

ALLEN, WALTER. "An Artist of the Thirties." *Folios of New Writing*, III (Spring 1941), 149–58. First article to deal extensively with Green's symbolism and his statement about "a gathering web of insinuations."

———. *The Modern Novel in Britain and the United States*. New York: E. P. Dutton, 1964. Material about Green assembles Allen's earlier material in a helpful form.

ANON. "The Bookman's Diary." *The Bookman* [London], LXXVI (June 1929), 167–69. Rare example of adverse contemporary criticism of *Living*.

BAIN, BRUCE. "Henry Green: The Man and His Work." *World Review*, No. 3 (May 1949), 55–58, 80. Contains both biographical and critical information; discusses style, imagery, symbolism.

BASSOFF, BRUCE. "Prose Consciousness in the Novels of Henry Green." *Language and Style*, V (1972), 276–86. Excellent study of Green as a prose stylist.

———. *Toward Loving: The Poetics of the Novel and the Practice of Henry Green*. Columbia: University of South Carolina Press, 1975. Helpful study of novel theory in general and of the novel *Loving* in particular.

BROGAN, D. W. "Recent Fiction." *New Republic*, XLIX (December 29, 1926), 174. Positive contemporary review of *Blindness*.

BURGESS, ANTHONY. *The Novel Now*. New York: W. W. Norton, 1967. Appreciative. One novelist describing the poetic elements in the prose of another novelist.

COSMAN, MAX. "The Elusive Henry Green." *Commonweal*, LXXII (September 9, 1960), 472, 474–75. Attempts to catch glimpses of Green in his novels.

DAVIDSON, BARBARA. "The World of *Loving*." *Wisconsin Studies in Contemporary Literature*, II (Winter 1961), 65–78. Thoroughgoing study of art and love in *Loving*.

DENNIS, NIGEL. "The Double Life of Henry Green." *Life*, XXXIII (August 4, 1952), 83–94. Useful article on Green, the man and author.

GARNETT, DAVID. "Books in General." *New Statesman and Nation*, XVIII (October 7, 1939), 489. Discussion of the comedy and seriousness of *Party Going*.

GILL, BRENDON. "Something." *The New Yorker*, XXVI (March 25, 1950), 103–104. With the premise that *Nothing* is better than something, Gill discusses the comedy of "ruthless self-regard."

HALL, JAMES. *The Tragic Comedians: Seven Modern British Novelists*. Bloomington: Indiana University Press, 1963. Contains an analysis of the pleasure-and-pain theme in Green's novels.

HART, CLIVE. "The Structure and Technique of *Party Going*." *Yearbook of English Studies*, I (1971), 185–99. Useful analysis of the organic technique of Green, the "invisible artist."

HILTON, JAMES. "Two More by Mr. Green." *New York Herald Tribune Book Review*, December 31, 1950, 4. Discusses the poetic elements in *Caught* and *Concluding*.

JOHNSON, BRUCE. "Henry Green's Comic Symbolism." *Ball State University Forum*, VI (Autumn 1965), 29–35. Anecdotal and allusive discussion of Green's synthesis of humor and symbolism.

LABOR, EARLE. "Henry Green's Web of Loving." *Critique*, IV (Fall-Winter 1960–61), 29–40. Perceptive study of loving in *Loving*.

LEHMANN, JOHN. *I Am My Brother*. New York: Reynal and Company, 1960. Contains a helpful view of Green by his publisher and friend. This and the other two volumes of Lehmann's autobiography have been published in one volume entitled *In My Own Time*. Boston: Little, Brown, 1969.

MELCHIORI, GIORGIO. *The Tightrope Walkers*. London: Routledge and Kegan Paul, 1956. Excellent study of Green as contemporary artist.

PAGE, NORMAN. *Speech in the English Novel*. London: Longmans Group Ltd., 1973. Speech in fiction and its relationship to real conversation with a case study of *Doting*.

PRITCHETT, V. S. "Green on Doting." *The New Yorker*, XXVIII (May 17, 1952), 137–42. One of several Pritchett articles on Green, this one emphasizes the characterization in *Doting*.

ROSS, ALAN. "Green, with Envy." *The London Magazine*, VI (April 1959), 18–24. Interview with Green emphasizing his themes of disintegration and dissolution.

RUSSELL, JOHN. *Henry Green: Nine Novels and an Unpacked Bag*. New Brunswick, New Jersey: Rutgers University Press, 1960. Excellent book-length study of Green's writing.

———. "There It Is." *The Kenyon Review*, XXVI (Summer 1964), 433–65. Long article on Green since his retirement after visits with him.

RYF, ROBERT S. *Henry Green*. New York: Columbia University Press, 1967.

No. 29 of Columbia Essays on Modern Writers. Quite useful as a long introductory essay.

SCOTT, J. D. "New Novels." *New Statesman and Nation*, XLIII (May 10, 1952), 564, 566. On Green's failure to advance with his last novel.

SHAPIRO, STEPHEN A. "Henry Green's *Back*: The Presence of the Past." *Critique: Studies in Modern Fiction*, VII (Spring 1964), 87–96. Perceptive analysis of *Back*.

SNOW, C. P. "Books and Writers." *Spectator*, CLXXXV (September 27, 1950), 320. Negative view of Green's theory of the novel.

SOUTHERN, TERRY. "The Art of Fiction XXII: Henry Green." *The Paris Review*, V (Summer 1958), 61–77. Excellent interview.

STOKES, EDWARD. *The Novels of Henry Green*. London: The Hogarth Press, 1959. First book-length study of Green, especially detailed on style.

TAYLOR, DONALD S. "Catalytic Rhetoric: Henry Green's Theory of the Modern Novel." *Criticism*, VII (Winter 1965), 81–99. Excellent analysis of Green's personal theory of the novel.

TINDALL, WILLIAM YORK. *The Literary Symbol*. Bloomington: Indiana University Press, 1955. Includes Green's use of symbols.

TOYNBEE, PHILIP. "The Novels of Henry Green." *Partisan Review*, XVI (May 1949), 487–97. Discusses Green as "a terrorist of language."

WEATHERHEAD, A. KINGSLEY. *A Reading of Henry Green*. Seattle: University of Washington Press, 1961. Interpretive work which emphasizes the self-creative drive of Green's characters.

WEAVER, ROBERT L. "The Novels of Henry Green." *The Canadian Forum*, XXX (January 1951), 227–28, 230–31. Discusses Green as a minor writer.

WELTY, EUDORA. "Henry Green: A Novelist of the Imagination." *The Texas Quarterly*, IV (Autumn 1961), 246–56. Immensely appreciative discussion of Green the novelist.

Index

153